P9-DDE-858

On a rare day of partial clearing clouds separate to reveal the Maritime Northwest. On the east, the Cascade Range protects it from the thirsty Plateau. On the west is the Pacific.

Southward the Siskiyous and Trinity Alps palisade the Maritime Northwest against the bare brown hills and burning plains of California. Northward, though maritime climate persists, agriculture ceases, turned back by mountains that rise from the surf.

Eureka
CAPE MENDOCINO
SHASTA
Klamath
Medford
Crescent City
Grant's Pass
Roseburg
Rogue
CAPE BLANCO
Umpqua
Coos Bay
Willamette
SISTERS
Eugene
Corvallis
JEFFERSON
Salem
HOOD
Portland
Columbia
ADAMS
ST. HELENS
Longview
Astoria
Cowlitz
RAINIER
Olympia
Tacoma
Puget Sound
Seattle
Aberdeen
Everett
Hood Canal
GLACIER PK.
OLYMPICS
Skagit
Bellingham
BAKER
Strait of Juan de Fuca
Victoria
CAPE FLATTERY
Fraser
Strait
Vancouver
of
Georgia
VANCOUVER ISLAND
Nootka Sound
CAPE COOK
Queen Charlotte Strait
CAPE SCOTT
S
E
W
R BENSON

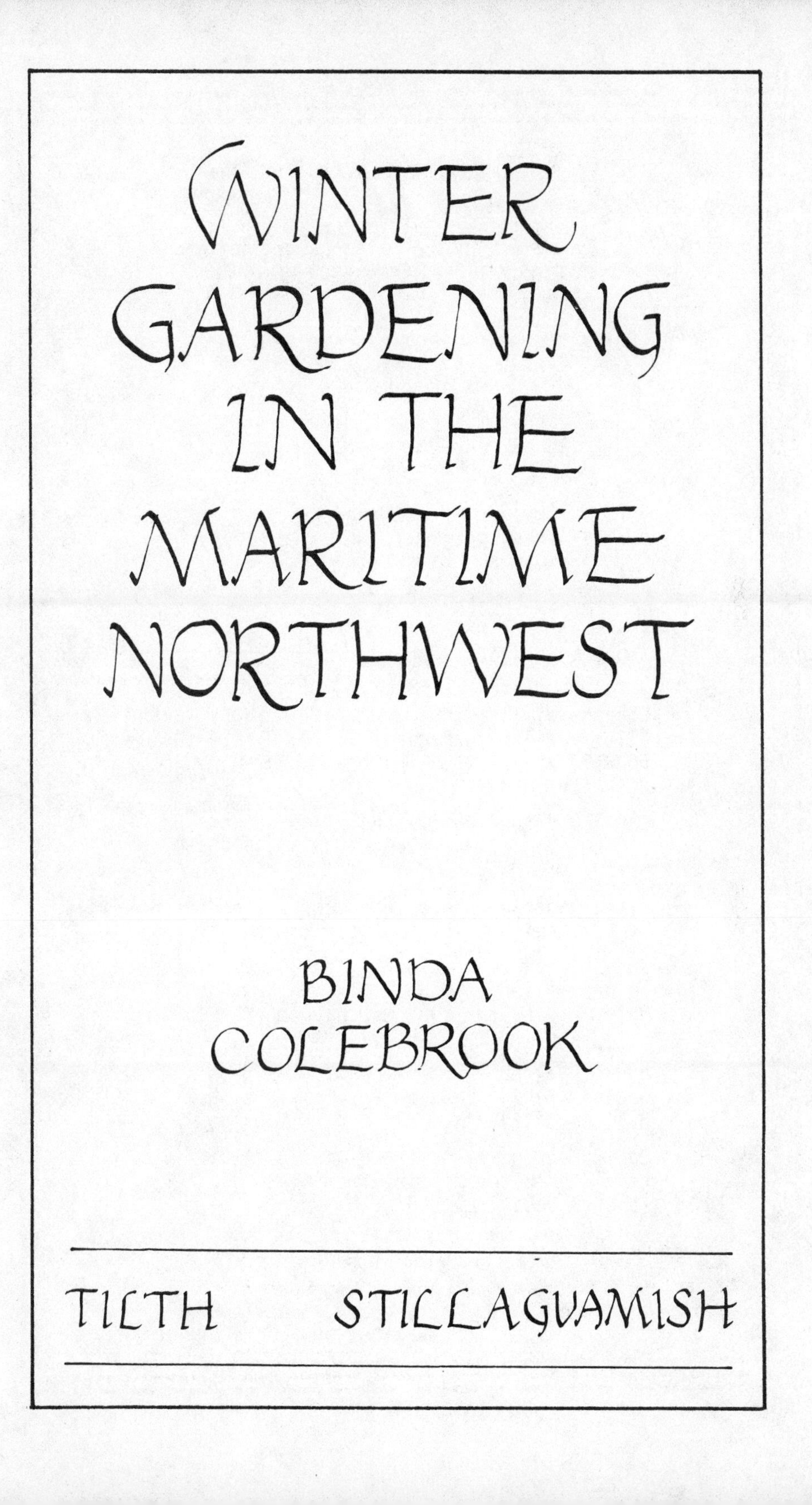
WINTER GARDENING IN THE MARITIME NORTHWEST

BINDA COLEBROOK

TILTH STILLAGUAMISH

WINTER GARDENING IN THE MARITIME NORTHWEST

© November 1977 by Binda Colebrook

Published by the Tilth Association
Rt 2, Box 190-A, Arlington WA 98223

Production & Editing by Mark Musick
Rhoda Epstein and Steve Johnson

Graphics by Roberto Williamson
Carol Oberton, Bob Benson
Kari Berger

First printing, November, 1977
Second printing, April, 1978
Third printing, October, 1978

Credits

Bob Benson—map of the maritime northwest, page 2

Roberto Williamson—cover, calligraphy, and illustrations on pages 1,36,38,39,40,44,45, 56,62,67,69,72,75,76,77,79,83,84,87,89,92,93,94,95, 98,99,106,110,114

Carol Oberton—charts and illustrations on pages 16,18,21,24,25,29,30,33,34,46,48,50, 53,59,70,85,91

Diane Hagaman—photo, back cover: reprinted by permission of The Seattle Times

Jody Aliesan—"Waiting", page 35; reprinted by permission from Soul Claiming, 1974, Mulch Press, Box 598, Northampton MA 01060

Peter Warshall—quoted from Transformation I, page 108; reprinted by permission from Shelter, 1973, Shelter Publications, Box 297, Bolinas CA 94924

David MacKenzie—quote, pages 117-118; reprinted by permission from Goat Husbandry, Faber & Faber, London

Typeset on an IBM Selectric II
Printed at AdPro, Lynnwood WA
Bound at Bayles Bindery, Seattle WA
ISBN 0-931380-00-6

Dedication

For the mist people, for the fish people,
for the wave people and the rock people.
For the madrone people and the fern people.
For the cloud people and the wind people,
the gull people and the crow people. For
the owl people and the hawk people, the
grass people and the buttercup people, for
the clod people and the worm people, the
beetle people and the fly people. For the
slug people and the duck people, the sheep
people and the goat people. The cabbage
and the rose people. For the mouse people
and the house people.

All my relations, all my relations.

Acknowledgements

My list of acknowledgements is long. It starts with my mother, Joan Colebrook, who passed on to me her love of gardening and cooking, and some of her sense of poetics and prose.

Thanks and appreciation are also due to: Grant Cottam, Hugh Iltis, and other teachers at the University of Wisconsin-Madison for imparting a sense of ecology; Meghan McComisky for sharing her garden in Leschi; Bob Gill for my first lesson in winter gardening; Rick Erickson, Tom Ruel, and members of the Puget Consumers' Coop board of trustees for the initial grant which made the Winter Garden Project possible.

I also wish to thank all the participants in the Winter Garden Project, and most especially Myrna Twomey, Dar Rundberg, Rosemary Perdue, Gabriel, and Gary Franco; Nancy Peacock for editing and illustrating articles for the PCC newsletter; Forest Glenn Roth of the Abundant Life Seed Foundation for answering questions about seeds, Gerard Vreeburg of the University of Washington Drug Garden for aid in identifying various herbs and seed sources; and Woody and Becky Deryckx for inviting me to Pragtree Farm, and for being generous sources of information on homesteading and agriculture.

My thanks also go to Rachel Deryckx for being such a fine friend to my son, Dorje, and to Dorje for sharing his love, joy and support; to all those who spent time with him while I worked; to Davis Straub for showing me how to transplant cabbages by the hundreds; to the Evergreen Land Trust for making Pragtree Farm available; to the land of Pragtree for sheltering my body and soul for a year and a half; to the South Fork of the Stillaguamish River for just being there; to Larry and Sherry Johnson and Jerry Firnstahl for being such good country neighbors; and to Mark Musick for his patience, support, and friendship.

Publication of this first edition of WINTER GARDENING IN THE MARITIME NORTHWEST was made possible by a loan from the Corner Green Grocery Collective, and a loan and a grant from the Puget Consumers' Cooperative. Elaine Davenport gave much helpful feedback on the first draft. Phil Andrus edited the Sources section and is helping with promotion; Nancy Windham is handling distribution. All proceeds from this book will go towards sponsoring future research on new approaches to agriculture in the Pacific Northwest.

Table of Contents

Foreword

I wrote this book for people who live in the Maritime Northwest and who would like to have more fresh vegetables growing outside in their garden during the winter months. It will be especially useful to people who have learned their gardening in a continental climate, who are not aware of the possibilities of a maritime climate, and hence close up their gardens from October till May.

It will also be useful to people who have grown up in and gardened in this mild environment, but who have not been aware of the many winter varieties and good seed sources available to them. I myself belong to the former group, and have only four and a half years experience growing vegetables through the winter. I had the courage to write this book only because I could not find any other single source to fully meet the needs of local gardeners.

The ideas in this book may more appropriately fall under the heading of "year-round gardening" but, in restricting it to *winter* gardening, I wanted to stress the uniqueness of our climate.

Most of us, even Northwest natives, come from a culture that practices the gardening and cooking techniques of a dry, cold continental climate. The United States is 3000 miles wide; by the time most settlers got across, maritime English and European gardening techniques were a faint memory at best. And of course, shortly after they got here, California took over the winter produce market.

We got spoiled, sped up, and moved into apartments, too busy doing other things to grow our own food and with less space to do it in. With the higher fossil fuel prices, and increased understanding of the nasty effects of all those chemicals in our food, many now realize the importance of improving our gardening ways.

In this book you will find a statement of principles of winter gardening and a list of the vegetables, herbs, and their varieties with which you can experiment. You will not find complete cultural directions for how to grow these plants. These directions are available in other books (listed under Sources) and I see no reason to duplicate them here.

Introduction

In the spring of 1971 I arrived in Seattle and, after finding shelter with friends, searched out the next most important thing to me—a spot in which to grow a garden. In fact I found two spots, one in the then new P Patch on 85th NE, and one behind the house I moved into on Capitol Hill. Both gardens were already growing plants, so I had the pleasure of just weeding and tending them without any of the anxieties of having to find out what grew well in this radically different part of the world (I'd come from the East Coast via Wisconsin).

I went away that fall and, coming back in December, found the Capitol Hill garden weedy and destitute of vegies. However, the P Patch, much to my surprise, had great lovely plants of kale and parsley scattered through it. With great delight I dug a few of both and took them home in a cardboard box. But before I had time to dig them in again, it started to snow.

That was an outstanding blizzard for Seattlites; it stayed on the ground for several weeks. When the snow melted, there were the plants, happily sitting in their dark safe container, fresh as the day I lifted them.

That was my introduction to the strange wonderful mild winters of the Pacific Northwest and, coming from Wisconsin, I was amazed. Seeing that the ground had never frozen, I dug some holes (in the process discovering a few of the summer's carrots, sweet and crisp as in July) and put in the kale and parsley. We ate them till May.

It might have been longer, but I moved to another house with an even better winter garden site. This one was in Leschi, by Lake Washington, and it was October. It was a little late for starting plants. But I went down to the Seattle Garden Center to talk to Bob Gill and there discovered that there was a dedicated group of people who made the effort to grow fresh vegetables all winter.

Bob sold me some onion sets, garlic and raab, gave me as much advice as he could, and I was on my way. The bulbs did well, but the raab was stunted by the wet, infertile soil I had chosen for it. I didn't yet have a firm grasp of the underlying principles of winter cropping, but those became more clear after a year or so. By the winter of '74-'75 I was able to produce all of my own winter vegetables on only 720 sq.ft. of moderately sunny ground..

In the spring of '75, Rick Erickson, then produce manager of the Puget Consumers' Coop (PCC), convinced me that I should find out what other gardeners were doing year-round, teach some classes, and see if there were commercial possibilities for farmers to produce winter vegetables for the Coop. It was due to Rick's and the Coop's commitment to having fresh local produce available that PCC initiated the Winter Garden Project, and made this book possible.

By the fall of '75 there were fifteen participants in the Winter Garden Project, sharing ideas, successes and failures with me. Some were in Seattle, and the rest divided between Whidbey, Lopez, Orcas, and Port Townsend. We got some maximum/minimum thermometers (they record the highest and lowest temperatures of the day) to see at what point different varieties would freeze out, and I went around visiting the participant's gardens, observing what did and didn't happen.

I wouldn't want you to get the idea that this was anything fancy, or could be called "scientific" research. We were just a group of gardeners encouraging each other to be less dependent on trucked-in vegetables, figuring out when different varieties had to be sown, and enjoying the excitement of home-grown lettuce in January.

In the spring of '76 I moved out of the city to Pragtree Farm near Arlington, Washington. I spent a year and a half there working with folk who were growing vegetables on a commercial scale. This was very different from small-scale gardening. The farm is in the foothills of the Cascades, so the climate is much closer to continental than the Puget Sound Basin. This enabled me to test the hardiness of many varieties and gave me the beginnings of an understanding of what commercial farmers are up against.

While at the farm I also began to locate new cold-hardy varieties. Some of these were Asian, but most were from England and Europe. I also began to seek out comprehensive English gardening books and seed catalogues from the British Isles. Had I spoken other languages and had better contacts, I would have also sought out Japanese, Danish, Dutch, Belgian and French sources. In any case, the few books that I did get my hands on convinced me that the art of winter gardening is still alive in Britain and Europe.

There were also three local books that helped to reassure me that my explorations and efforts weren't foolish. The first was by Cecil Solly, *Growing Vegetables in the Pacific Northwest*. It was published during World War II, another time when people were needing to be more self-sufficient. Mr. Solly clearly had a garden that was productive year-round.

The second book was *The Food Lovers Garden*, written in 1970 by Angelo Pellegrini, who lives in Seattle's University District and who has one of the better gardens that I have seen locally. Mr. Pellegrini has a hearty Mediterranean orientation to food. His book is well worth reading, with much good cultural advice for spring, summer, and fall crops.

The third book was *Earth Market*, by Wendy Bender, a Canadian who lives on the coast of Vancouver Island, at approximately the same latitude as Mt. Vernon, Washington. Ms. Bender is a proponent of self-sufficiency in vegetables. She states her case well with illustrations from her own gardening experience.

I think that we should take a hint from these books and continue to develop our skills in growing our own food. We should also keep vegetable varieties extant by improving them and adapting them to our local conditions, thereby helping to develop our own regional garden flora.

This book is but a beginning; the art of winter cropping in this region is still in its infancy. Much is still to be learned from experimentation. I have tried to lay out the bare bones of the art and flesh them with what little I know, but you must continue the process.

Besides any technical information in this book, one of its primary purposes is to show you that with very little effort you can have more than enough green vegetables growing in your garden to feed you all winter long. Nine years out of ten.

You don't have to be an expert to do it. I wasn't when I started. You just have to be a good, adventuresome gardener.

The Principles of Winter Gardening

CLIMATE

The earth turns eastward round her poles. Our main wind comes to us from the west, across hours of ocean, damp and restless. That mass of ocean air gives us our climate, known as maritime, which prevails till over the Cascades. Here it gives generously of its water. The climate then becomes continental; dry, with extremes of temperature between summer and winter.

When I first came to Seattle it seemed to me that the weather in the Northwest was mostly the same, a steady hovering around 45°F and usually grey. Each season seemed endless. Spring took three to four months. Back east you were lucky to have it around for three weeks.

Some years summer came, an incredible month of continuous sun, but sometimes not—just an endless season of mist and rain, gradually turning cold enough to be winter. Especially near water and in the cities, freezes are very mild because of the moisture laden air. This steady state is rather like a refrigerator, slowing the hardier garden plants down but not killing them till January, if at all.

Western European gardeners, living with a similar climate for many more generations, evolved a hundred different winter varieties and as many techniques for making sure that they got their crop. They didn't have California, trucking systems, and freezers to fall back on, but they used the plant resources of three continents to provide their winter vegetables.

Although some years the "Hunger Gap" (February to April) was longer than others, they almost always would have something green for a salad or the pot. Many of these varieties and techniques have succumbed to modern technology, but enough is left to still see the pattern. It is a pattern which we can follow.

Site

A proper site and appropriate soil conditions are the foundation of a productive winter garden.

The best site is a gentle slope on the south side of a hill or a building. Ideally, it would be a site you could terrace, with wind protection close enough to make a difference but not too close to block the sun.

A building reflects and holds heat; slope aids in drainage; terraces make a warm microclimate; and wind protection allows that pocket of warm air to stay where it has developed.

Usually the best place for the winter garden is also a good sunbathing spot, so let that be your guide. When the sun comes out for a week during those frequent January-February highs you should be able to work comfortably in shorts and a shirt in the perfect site. I did in Leschi, though just around the corner it was still winter. That extra warmth means extra growth on your broccoli, corn salad, Brussels sprouts, etc., and hence more food. It also means warmer temperatures at night and can make the difference between losing your plants to freezes or not.

Of course, if you live in the city, and your few choices for a garden don't include a particularly sunny spot (less than half a day of sun), then you may have to limit the kinds of vegetables you will grow. Better to have lots of spinach, lettuce and corn salad, than cabbages that don't make it, especially if you are more likely to eat the former raw, and hence maximize your nutrition.

You can be ingenious and use reflecting surfaces and such. There is some good information on this in the Ortho booklet, *Weather Wise Gardening*, sold at chain hardware stores. Just remember they are pushing plastics and other petrochemical products. Though I can think of less rational places to use plastic than in your garden, still it's a good idea to limit your use of environmentally pernicious substances.

If your only sunny spot faces onto a street, beware. Traffic exhaust will be coating your plants, soil and, what's worse, your lungs with lead and other nasties. My best advice would be to move, but if you can't, be sure to wash your food well. Pollution from factories is just as bad, of course, but in the Puget Sound Basin it tends to be less common except downwind of the Tacoma smelter and the Everett pulp mills.

If you live in the exurbs or country you might have lots of space but no warm microclimate. Then I think it's worth your while to make a walled garden out of whatever material you can scrounge.

The warmest spot on a farm or exurban home is the south side of the house, which traditionally con- the perennial flower bed. If you like flowers that's a hard thing to give up. Maybe you can fit broccoli and onion greens in amongst the asters. Be careful though, many garden flowers and bulbs are poisonous, and you wouldn't want to eat a tulip bulb thinking it was an onion.

Drainage, of both water and air, is another very important aspect of a site. Low spots are poor for winter gardens. They collect cold air (hence early frosts) as well as water. Of course, you can have water problems in the middle of a slope, and if so you have to do something about the drainage. A wet soil will be too cold for good growth and it will suffocate your plants. They need air around their roots.

Breaking up the subsoil will sometimes do the trick, especially if you work in a lot of humus. But if there is a serious impediment, like clay or asphalt, you may want to build raised beds.

You can also have air drainage problems in the middle of a slope if you have a barrier to the free flow of air. A tight fence down hill of your garden will catch the freezing air instead of letting it pass on by. Use an open fence, or a hedge.

Soil

The perfect soil for a winter garden is dark, full of humus, sandy, and well drained. This kind of soil warms up fast, holds heat longer, won't freeze as easily, and won't hold water excessively during long rainy spells. If your summer garden is in a low spot with heavy rich soils that hold water during summer droughts, you will probably not want to try and change its nature for a winter garden. Seek some other part of your land to make the winter site.

Compost, worked into the soil before late summer plantings of the leafy greens, will hold some extra warmth in the soil as it further decomposes. It will also enrich it. If you are a year-round gardener you are removing organic matter from the soil most of time, and so you have to be extra careful to replace it by composting and other methods, such as green manuring.

A green manure is a crop that is planted in ground that otherwise would be idle, and then is disced or dug in two to three weeks before sowing and left to decompose. Many people use rototillers for this purpose, but I think they scramble the soil structure so badly that, on a small site, you are better off taking time to do this by hand.

Green manuring is better than mulching in winter because the activity of the roots both adds organic matter and keeps nutrients in the root area where they aren't leached by the endless rain.

There are many good green manure crops, including legumes, grasses and herbs, but probably the best for winter are annual rye and vetch, or annual rye and Austrian winter peas.[1] Rye will germinate down to 40°F at least, and will continue to grow at 32°F. Winter peas can usually be sown as late as the end of October, though earlier sowings will add more nitrogen to the soil (especially if you have remembered to add inoculant for nitrogen fixing bacteria). Vetch planted by August has been shown to contribute 100 lbs. of nitrogen per acre to the soil.[2]

All this costs you some thought at first, and the price of the seed, but in the end it is far less expensive than store bought manure, and less work than hauling manure and making compost. However, you should make compost too; let nothing be wasted from your household. Add to your compost any herbs and weeds you can find, for these draw up nutrients from the soil in a way that most vegetables cannot; comfrey, nettles, docks, plantain, yarrow, dandelions, anything in fact but bindweed, blackberries, buttercup and quackgrass.

Rotations

Another essential practice for the year-round gardener is rotating crops by family. Until recently this subject puzzled me a lot. Though I made efforts to comply with certain dire warnings such as NEVER GROW CABBAGES IN THE SAME PLACE TWICE IN A ROW, or DON'T FOLLOW POTATOES WITH TOMATOES, I didn't have a very good scope of a total system.

Then I got a hold of John and Sally Seymour's book, *Farming for Self-Sufficiency*, (see page 126) and finally began to understand that gardening rotations are based on soil requirements and disease patterns of common vegetables, especially the brassicas, (e.g. cabbage, broccoli, cauliflower, kale, etc.) and the solanaceous plants (e.g. potatoes). The four-year rotation, which they describe in Chapter 14 of their book goes as follows:

SEYMOUR ROTATION

(apply aged manure or compost)
1 potatoes
(lime after potato harvest)
2 brassicas
3 peas and beans
4 roots
(then you start all over again)

You should read the chapter in the Seymour book about this. It has a nice discussion of a calendar year in a Welsh garden. Basically, the idea is to enrich the soil with manure (they call it muck) for the potatoes. Harvest them and then lime the soil, for potatoes don't grow well in alkaline soil.

Then plant brassicas, for they need lime (the parent plant of most of them, *Brassica oleracea*, having evolved on the chalk deposits of England), and then go on with peas and beans which also like lime, following last with the roots that like a well dug soil, but don't handle manure well.

LD HILLS ROTATION

(apply aged manure or compost)
1 potatoes
(lime after potato harvest)
2 peas and beans
3 brassicas
4 roots
(then you start all over again)

This is a slightly different rotation, suggested by LD Hills who is the head of the Henry R. Doubleday Research Association (see page 124), based on findings that lime takes a year to really incorporate into the soil. This is especially important if you are dealing with the fungus disease clubroot which is suppressed by lime. I did come across clubroot once in Seattle, and also at Pragtree Farm. It is potentially a bad problem, so it's best to practice preventive medicine, in this case, rotations and liming your soil, especially in small gardens.

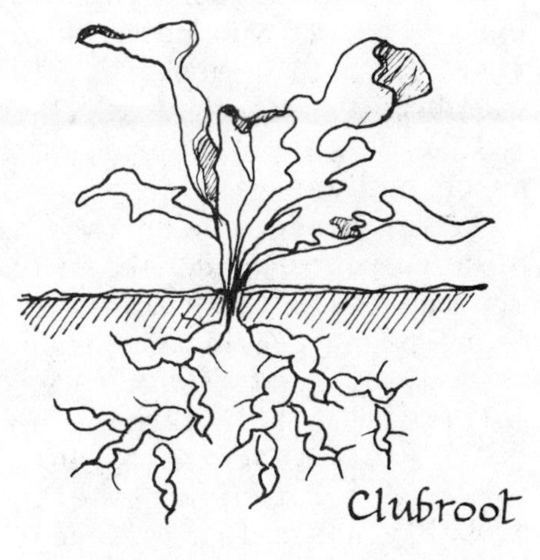
Clubroot

A virtue of following peas and beans with brassicas (especially the leafy ones) is that they get the added benefit of the nitrogen that the legumes have fixed. Elaine Davenport (a founder of the Tilth Association) observed on the European Farm Tour* in 1976 that many organic gardeners and farmers grew leafy brassicas after legumes to use this fertilizer.

You could slip any other noncruciferous leafy green in after the legumes, as long as it didn't interfere with the overall rotation. This might include lettuce, chard, spinach, celery, corn salad, etc. according to season. Hills has illustrated a series of rather complex schemes to fit all these other vegetables into the basic rotation in his *Grow Your Own Fruits & Vegetables* (see page 124)

---

*Sponsored each year by Elliot Coleman of the Small Farm Research Association, Harborside, Maine 04910.

To tell the truth, these are very hard for me to follow. I don't have a very mathematical mind and blunder through rotation planning each year hoping for the best.

It never comes out *quite* how you planned it anyhow. Vegetables are often not ready to take out when you need to put the next plants in according to the map, so it's best to work out your own variations.

Organic?

I think organic gardening is the only way to go, but I won't say you can't crop all year with store bought chemical fertilizers because I don't know; I've never tried it. If you do it successfully for more than five years, let me know, I'd be interested. I still wouldn't try it though. I don't think it's necessary, and from what I've read, it's actually harmful as well as being expensive.

Also, since winter is a time of greater stress for plants, you should make sure your cultural conditions are the best. In this case I suspect that "best" means plenty of humus (organic matter) and a vital micro flora and fauna. You don't come by those with artificial fertilizers!

If you are new to organic gardening and don't want to spend a lot of money on books, your public library probably has a fairly decent number of books available. In Seattle, ask for the bibliography of the Public Library's holdings, *Organic Vegetable Gardening in the City*. Also see the sources section in back of this book.

I'm often asked about intensive methods and companion planting in relation to winter crops, so I will discuss my feelings on these here.

In general, I think that intensive bed planting is a good technique, saves space, is better for the root systems, etc. I plant a lot of my vegetables this way. Most people, however, only know of it through Jeavons' book, *How to Grow More Vegetables*..., as the "Biodynamic/ French Intensive" method. First, I think if you want to know about Bio-dynamics you should read some of their literature directly (see page 125). It's very interesting.

Second, I wonder about the French part. Intensive bed planting is practiced all over Europe as well as in Asia.

These are probably picky criticisms. A more important one is that the spacings are not appropriate for the Maritime Northwest, especially for winter, and therefore you cannot expect the yields Jeavons reports. As long as you remember to increase plant spacings, it would be worthwhile for you to read the book and incorporate whatever seems useful into your own methods of gardening.

As to companion planting, most lists I've seen (all apparently copied from the Philbrick & Gregg book, *Companion Plants—and how to use them*[4]) take it as a matter of fact. However, to my knowledge, this year for the first time Philbrick's & Gregg's theories are being tested by other gardeners in a controlled way. The HR Doubleday Research Association is organizing this. If you are interested you might want to contact them and see if you can contribute.

I'm not one to demand that everything be proven by "science". Quite the opposite. It's just that I get bored by hearing people endlessly repeat what plants "like" other plants, and not even credit Philbrick and Gregg who themselves request feedback from other gardeners on their experiences. Further, following those lists slavishly, instead of making your own experiments and observations in your own locale is quite contrary, I feel, to the practice of good gardening. Or good living.

Further, my feelings about our common vegetables is that, since they are derived from weeds which have associated with people and their manure heaps for thousands of years, they are by nature fairly flexible in their associations and, rather like city folk, can live cheek and jowl with their neighbors and not suffer unduly.

This is not to say, of course, that in their wild state they don't form natural associations of mutual benefit; undoubtedly they do. I just don't know of any good botanical (ecological) studies on this. Besides, your garden, and the varieties you sow are not terribly close to the "wild" state.

The Elements

I know it's hard for us sun loving humans not to miss the sun and not to complain about the damp. So often I hear people expressing one-sided feelings about the weather. Sun is most often "good". When rain and wind come it is a "bad" day, "bad weather".

I think we need to recognize and welcome rain and wind. They are Water and Air, those elements whose nature is to flow and mediate. They make glorious living patterns over the body of the Earth, swirling over the islands of the Sound. If we are to reachieve a holistic way of life, we would best begin by truly perceiving that Air, Water and Fire, in their flowing, unite with Earth and create life.

We live on the western coast of our continent, in an environment that is more subtle and fluid than that which lies down weather, to the east of us.

I see the people here as open hearted and flexible. I hardly think this quality would be decreased by growing our food through wet and cold and feeding our bodies with the stuff of our environment.

In loving ourselves and this bit of earth we share, we all stand to gain.

Wind

No matter how good a site you have in other respects, if the wind can blow away the warm air that has been built up, it won't do the plants much good. There are two distances at which wind protection is useful: 1) very tall structures, trees, or a hill at a relatively far distance; and 2) really close low ones that include everything from the garden fence to boards, shingles, and cloches. With all of these, as the prevailing winds come from the south in this area (except when we are having a high), you have to make sure your wind protection doesn't block the low winter solstice sun.

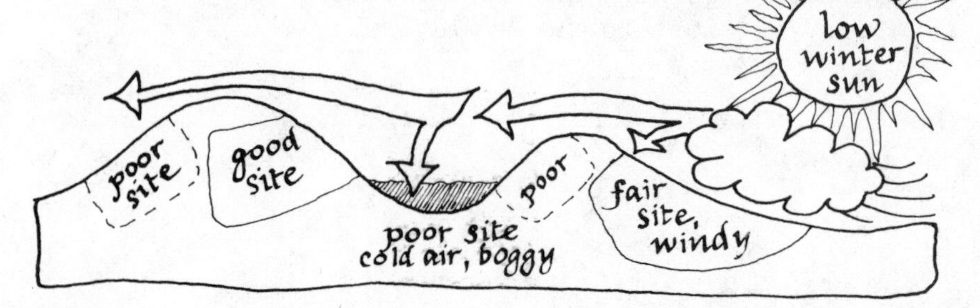

The following graphs show that a solid barrier only protects about eight times the height of the fence, and not very well at that due to air turbulence. A slatted fence or hedge makes a much more effective barrier to the wind, protecting up to sixteen times the height of the fence.[5]

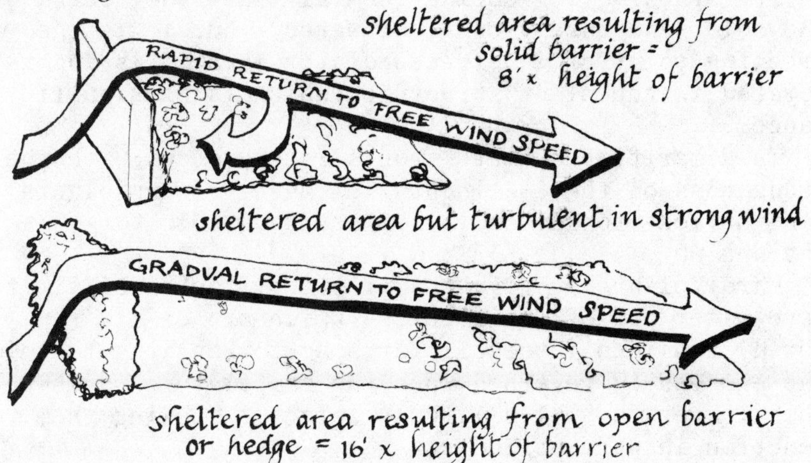

European gardens are often walled or hedged, and buildings, both there and in New England (where I came from) are often built in a complex that leaves a sheltered space in the middle. If you are in a situation where you can control the design of your house and outbuildings, I strongly suggest you form such a complex. It's an energy saver all around. In the city or suburbs this protection happens automatically from the smallness of lots and the proximity of buildings.

In the New England countryside the buildings were usually built in one piece, but this is a fire hazard and should be avoided. Fences connecting buildings would serve just as well.

sheltered garden sites

Usually, wherever you live there is a place that you can find which will serve, or a structure you can build or grow to help break the wind. If you do grow hedges, remember to use plants that are edible or medicinal, either for you or your stock (see Winter Crops for Livestock, page 115).

Wet and Cold

Wet and cold. It's important to talk about them together. Usually when people think of the plants in their gardens dying during the fall they only think of the cold, and rarely consider water. But it is the freezing point of water, especially when it is incorporated in the plant structure, which is of significance.

In a maritime climate frosts rarely occur with the suddenness of the continental climate, giving plants long periods to adjust. They are thus able to "harden up".

Hardy plants survive the frosts by their ability to move water out of their cells (which are easily ruptured) and into intercellular spaces when it gets cold. The process is reversed when the temperature warms up. This leaves the cells largely intact, allowing them to function in warm periods.

Further, this ability to move water back and forth is aided by certain chemicals, interestingly enough, abundant in seaweeds. This probably explains why so many people have reported increased hardiness after they have sprayed with seaweed emulsion, or actually mulched with seaweed.[7]

The winter gardener should take some precautionary steps to avoid losing plants to rot.

With mature plants, care must be taken to keep the lower leaves trimmed back, and with some delicate plants like lettuce, a drying mulch around their base is a help. Sawdust is okay, but wood chips or wood shavings are better.

Flower buds on cauliflower and broccoli are easily damaged, primarily from a combination of rain and frost. The leaves work well here for covering them.

Rot is also a problem with early spring crops. It is often helpful to temporarily cover early sowings of peas, favas and carrots if the season is excessively rainy. A simple thing like chicken wire covered with plastic will often provide sufficient protection.

Plants that have been overfed on water (and nitrogen) in the late summer and fall grow large and sappy. That is, their sap is diluted, they have trouble translocating enough water out of their cells, and they are therefore damaged during frosts.

While too much rain can be a hazard in the late summer, come winter it is more of a blessing because it retards frost. That is, water vapor in the air helps to maintain slightly higher temperatures in freezing weather. The latent heat in the vapor is returned to the air as water condenses in the form of frost. Thus, because maritime climates have such a high humidity, those early fall frosts when the plants are not yet completely hardened off are less damaging.

A further plus is those grey misty mornings we so often have, giving frozen plants time to thaw out gradually instead of subjecting them to bright sun and sudden wilting.

So stop complaining about the rain and mist and bless it instead—it's helping your garden!

Protection from the Elements

In general I prefer to focus on plants that can make it through the winter outside without any help or covering. I believe that extra work should be avoided, and coverings certainly require more work. Contraptions that you have to fool with (cold frame covers, burlap covers, sheds, greenhouses) take time. You have to be home to close them up if a sudden frost or storm threatens or open them if the sun shines. They cost money. They cut down on the amount of radiation a plant receives (which is little enough as it is in this climate!) and, unless you are very careful, they increase chances of rot.

Still, there are those crops, like lettuce, without which your diet might seem incomplete and sad. It is important, therefore, to create something to help you carry lettuce over the winter.

There are a wide range of possibilities, from the most simple (mulching, or throwing some wire and burlap over the plants) to the most complicated (expensive cloches and structures that just fall short of greenhouses). Use of protection devices *can* mean the difference between whether a plant just sits there or whether it produces extra growth (food!).

I will describe some protection devices and you can think about which ones are most suited for your situation.

Terraces

Just the structure of a terrace makes for a warmer microclimate, but the plants that will benefit from it will have to be low and hardy (corn salad, onion greens, spinach, etc.) unless you have a considerable slope and the risers are high enough to accommodate tall plants such as broccoli.

Terraces also warm up the soil, and that's half of the gain right there. Spring forcing carrots (March planting?) would do well in such an environment. You could staple a piece of plastic over the terrace to keep off the rain till the carrots were up.

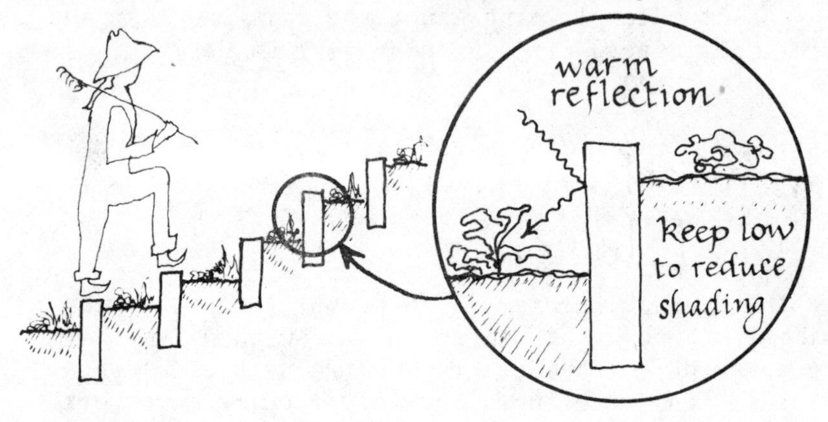

Remember that the warmest spot is right against the north riser, so don't put your path there. Build terraces so you can walk on and work from the risers, thus wasting no space.

Cloches

Cloche is a French word meaning bell, referring to the bell shaped jars that were originally used as hot caps put over tender plants early in the year to protect them from frost. The term expanded in meaning to include many different sizes and shapes of structures that could be put over individual plants in a row, or over the whole row (a barn cloche), and then stored when not in use.

At one point many gardeners, commercial and home, were using them for much of the winter. Originally they were made of glass and tended to break a lot. Now some are available in fiberglass and other longer lasting synthetics (see sources), but they are very expensive. Handy if you have the money, though.

Cold Frames

A cold frame is a more permanent structure than a cloche. It's placed on the earth facing south and has a glass cover. In colder climates matting, leaves, or rugs are often put over the glass, but here in the maritimes we rarely need that. In fact, most of the time you are better off (even in the foothills) leaving your cold frame uncovered; more radiation and better air circulation give better growth. I've noticed that even on cold nights, with the cover off, the inside of the frame was several degrees warmer than the outside (32°F instead of 28°F).

When it warms up in late February/early March, the increased heat in the frame means increased production. If you want to *eat* your lettuce rather than just keep it alive, covering the frame is all to the good. Lettuce is, in fact, the best thing to go in a cold frame.

One of the more enterprising gardeners at the 85th St. P Patch, in the first year of the project, built a structure for her winter lettuce that was sort of a cold frame (but not quite), sort of a rain fly (but not quite), and more besides; it had a reflector on the north wall. Thus it maximized radiation, protected plants from excessive rain, held in some heat by cutting down on radiation to the night sky and by shielding from the south winds with baffles, but allowed for air circulation by being open east and west.

This open quality was important; other project gardeners who built conventional type cold frames that

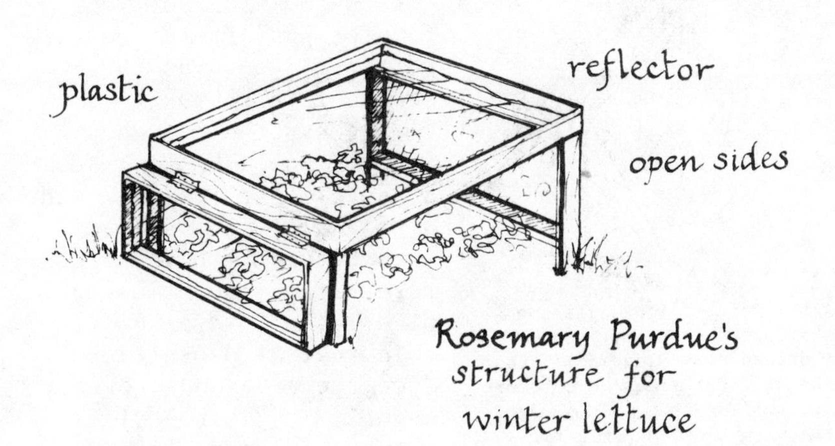

Rosemary Purdue's structure for winter lettuce

year lost many of their lettuce to rot. A conventional frame left *open* most of the time will work also; you just have to remember to close it during the colder times, especially clear nights.

Spring cabbages and broccolis can also be started in a cold frame. Start them in late August/early September, overwinter them in the frame, and then put them out at normal spacing in late February when the worst of the frosts have gone by. (See pages 63-72 for varieties to do this with.)

Hot Frames

Hot frames are just cold frames with a 3 ft. pit dug under them filled with manure for heat (preferably horse manure as it has the longest lasting, most even heat). Then a good 6-inch layer of soil is put on top in which you can plant the seeds.

You can sow a hot frame or hot shed full of carrots, lettuce, radishes, beets, and onion sets in late January, and be eating well from it in April. I have some friends who did that in Leschi and it worked wonderfully, even without a full day's sun due to trees and a hill.

Plastic Sheds

The advantages of building plastic sheds are that they can be made larger and seem to heat up better than cold frames. You can build a shed right over your winter lettuce, broccoli, cauliflower and spring cabbage and take them off when the weather gets warm. (Or put your tomatoes in after them... but that's outside the scope of this book.)

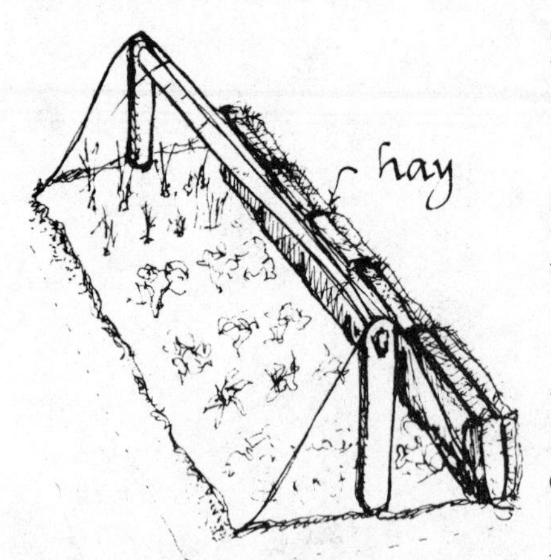

Example of a 4 foot tall shed constructed of 20 mil plastic stretched over ridge pole. South, east and west sides held secure with soil. North side secured with hay bales; movable for access.

I guess the only hesitancy I have about these sheds is that they are made of plastic, and as I've said before, I have strong reservations about using plastic. (I've also been told that it doesn't produce the greenhouse effect as well as glass.) It's quick and cheap, and therefore good as a first experiment, or an emergency temporary structure. If you find that it's successful, then you might want to make it out of more permanent material. But then, of course, it becomes a greenhouse.

Reflectors

Using a reflector depends on whether or not you want more light in the day and less heat at night or vice versa. If the back of your frame or shed or whatever is light colored or covered with foil of some sort, it will cast more light on the north side of your plants during the day. But by this very action it will not absorb heat, and hence not have it to radiate out into the frame during the night when the temperature drops.

If you are growing plants for leaf (spinach, corn salad, lettuce) you might want the *reflective* surface which will stimulate such growth. If you are growing broccolis or cauliflowers which you want to bud up (form a head) you might want the *absorptive* surface which will give a more even 24-hour heat, and encourage flower and fruit formation.

Timing

The question of *when* you sow different plants so that they are in a proper condition for fall, winter and early spring harvesting, is a complex one. One of the main problems is trying to outguess the weather because an early or late fall will alter when a crop will produce, especially with the brassicas. What's good for the corn ain't so good for the cabbages.

You have to *intuit* the weather each year. It doesn't do much good to go by those mythical first and last frost dates that the Extension and Weather services are so fond of, and the tv is only of general help. You have to add up the data in your own computer (that's your head) and work from your feelings about what kind of a season it is, and how it's going to end up.

If you feel insecure about doing this for any number of good reasons, try successions. You will no doubt already be sowing successions of quick crops, such as lettuce, for your summer edibles. Well, try it for your winter ones. If you aren't sure about whether to plant your St. Valentine broccoli in early, mid or late June for a February crop, try early and late plantings, label well, and record what happens. If you keep these records, along with a descriptive paragraph about what the weather was like that year, you will have an invaluable record of your microsite and the timing you can follow to get crops.

Another aid to judging when to sow is understanding the topography of your site. This is because the microclimate of your particular area may differ radically from one that is in the same latitude and longitude, but which has different topographical features. In other words, within a certain range, rainshadow, closeness to water or mountains, elevations, etc. will be more important than degrees of latitude north or south.

Below is a chart to be used in conjunction with the Winter Gardening Calendar (see page 60) for visualizing the growing season.

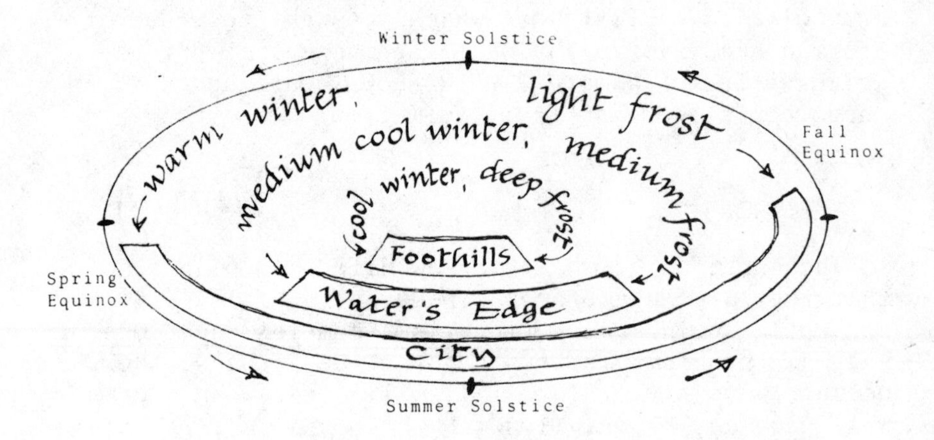

The chart is based on the climate of the Seattle area. If you live much south (say the Willamette Valley) or north (Vancouver Island), you will have to add or subtract a week or two at the most. In any case you will always have some leeway, and for some plants it is quite wide.

I've sown parsnips as early as March and as late as June and still gotten crops—just different sizes! On quick crops (such as spinach or lettuce) the sowing range, especially for fall and winter, is much narrower. The crops have to be given time (or a number of warm days) for them to be the size or state of maturity that you want them to be.

For example, say you want to plant Winterkeeper beets from Stokes. These are big rooted beets with fine sweet greens. For the Puget Sound area you have to plant them around the summer solstice (June 21) to get large roots. But you have several weeks latitude on either side of this. Say you are too busy, and miss the June and early July plantings. Should you bother? Is it too late? Well, this somewhat depends on whether you are more interested in greens or roots. If it's greens, or if small roots will do just as well, you're not too late.

Some crops, like Chinese cabbage, are much more precise. They are more acutely affected by day length, and you have maybe two weeks to get them in the ground.

The chart below illustrates how much leeway you have in sowing many different crops in different microclimates, using the examples of turnips and spinach.

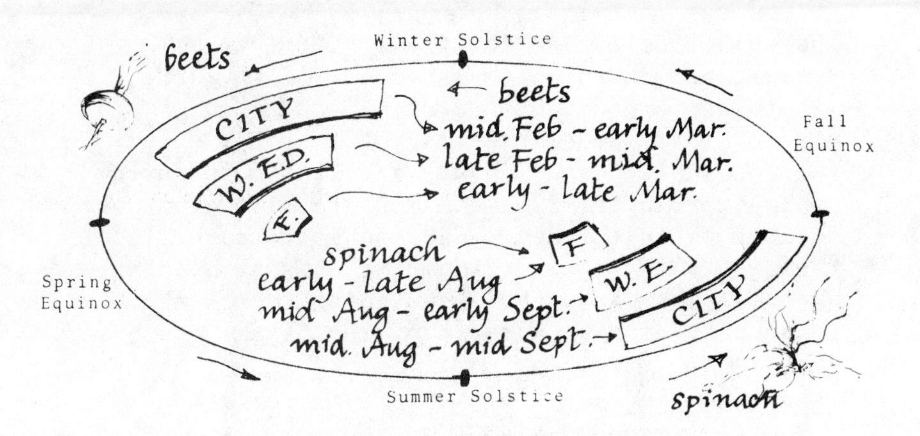

When you are looking in English seed catalogues, you will notice that their sowing dates for some brassicas are different than the ones I have given in the Winter Gardening Calendar. This is because if you sow when they suggest you would lose many of the plants to root fly maggot unless you used some form of protection (see page 48). The best way to find out when *you* need to plant these slow growing plants in order for them to crop when you want them to is to experiment with successions of several plantings over a month or so.

This is the kind of adjustment you have to make when you start using seed and cultural directions from

8,000 miles away and five to ten degrees latitude north of here, even if we do have a basically similar climate. In other words, we all have to do a lot of experimenting before we can come up with our own Maritime Northwest version of year-round gardening!

Finally, a lot of plants need to be planted in July and August, a busy time for most gardeners. In fact, most gardeners who participated in the Winter Garden Project said this was one of their greatest hassles. They didn't appreciate the pressure of having to deal with seeds and young plants throughout the summer when there's so much else to do. I certainly know how they feel! In the summer of '76, when I was trying out many different varieties, I got burnt out very quickly. My main suggestion in handling this problem is to *limit the amount of summer sown varieties in your garden*.

Because I value my peace of mind as much as I do fresh greens for the winter, one of the solutions I have for the summer overload problem is to get things organized. First, I try to order seeds in late winter for the *whole year*. Then, after the main spring sowings are over, I make a monthly file of my seed packets so that I don't have to go through all of them every month to decide which has to be planted when. I just know that I am going to sow the seeds in each section at a certain time of the month and that is it.

Waiting

Winter is shorter when you know a garden
and can still pull beets in early December.
Even, after everything's turned under
long nights are hours of rest, not death,
earned sleep after the land's labor

when kitchen tables bear seed packets,
almanacs, sketches,
when conversation
conjures up a tangled trellis of peas
before the first one plumps in a furrow.

That day apple twigs are already knobbier,
crocus tips slice old mulch,
                                        February
is already spring.

Robins watch the hoe.

Jody Aliesan

Picking Your Produce

A great deal of the art of winter cropping lies in knowing when and how to pick your plants. The first rule is don't plant more than you can eat. You will have to allow some extra for frost damage, but its not that much more.

The second rule is to spend the necessary time every week to keep the various plants trimmed back so there aren't a lot of yellowing mushy leaves lying around and inviting rot. Generally speaking, the older the leaves, the more susceptible to damage they are. Further, picking those older leaves stimulates the core or crown of the plant to produce more growth. This is very obvious in the kales and cabbages. When you take the bottom leaves from a kale plant it will start to send off shoots from just above the leaf scar.

If you pick the kale plants clean in late October or early November, then they will have some time before the winter solstice and the greatest cold to lay in an abundance of young and tender growth. Then they will just stand till mid-February when they start to grow again, stimulated by increasing light and warmth.

Cabbages can be dealt with in a similar manner. Forest Glenn Roth and his household in Seattle always had a large number of second year cabbages happily producing sprouts for them. They did this by picking outer leaves, buds, and sprouts, but leaving the stem in the ground.

You can even do this with cabbage from which you have cut the main head. In a few weeks, if you leave the stem in place, it will start to send up cabbagelets which taste just as good as the original heads.

For the other vegetables you have to think ahead and use your common senses—eyes, nose, and mouth. For instance, unless you have an excess of vegetables such as lettuce, spinach or kale, you won't want to pick the whole plant, just the lower leaves and sprouts. Using this procedure you can keep one plant producing for a long time.

At some point you will want to shift over to picking the whole plant. For instance, with corn salad, most of the time you will be picking the outer leaves of many plants, and not having a very great amount for your salads or sandwiches. But when the plants start shooting up late in March and getting crowded, you can take whole ones to feast on, leaving more space for the others.

Sometimes a little imagination is necessary to recognize a healthy red cabbage salad under some frosted slimy leaves, or a stir-fry in those weird elongated almost flowering Brussels sprouts. So the supermarkets don't sell edible flowers; does that mean you can't eat them? Or that they don't taste outrageously good in a salad?

There are heaps of cookbooks you could read, but I don't think you really need them. Just go into your garden in a February hunger, with a basket and a knife, and you'll find lots of food.

Eating It

Start eating right there in the garden. If live food is as healthy as people say, then it's hard to get any fresher than that.

However, once you get to the kitchen many of the winter hardy plants may be new to you and your family, so it's important to seek out recipes that show them off to their best. If you overcook them or yield to the temptation to always serve them in the same way, they will quickly become boring. That path leads back to the supermarket bins of expensive, unvital vegetables. LD Hills has some good recipes, and so does Wendy Bender (see page 124). Rombauer's *Joy of Cooking*, that marvelous kitchen standby, even has salsify recipes!

Substitution works well, too. If you can't find something new to do with raab or kale, and it's all you've got left in the garden, just think of a gourmet sauce that's good over some other vegetable and use that.

Some vegetables have substances in them that you don't want to overconsume. Beets, Swiss chard, French sorrel, and spinach are all high in oxalic acid which interferes with the calcium metabolism, so go easy on them. It's in rhubarb also, in another form, which is why the leaves are poisonous and why you shouldn't eat the stalks too late in the year; the oxalic acid concentrations build up.

Also, since a good proportion of the winter vegetables are brassicas, you should be aware that many if not all of these contain a substance which interferes with the action of thyroxine.[6] This substance is less active in the cool season in the plants, but it has, in Eastern Europe and Tasmania at least, been implicated in the formation of goiter. In Eastern Europe it was probably due to the lack of any vegetables other than the cabbage family, and in Tasmania it was probably due to milk cows being overstocked on pastures and therefore being excessively fed cruciferous supplements (e.g., kale and turnips). Apparently an excess of the thyroxine depressing substance came through in the milk to directly affect humans.

You shouldn't have any problem if you eat other vegetables, and your milk animals, if you have any, are fed with other greens, pasture and hay, in addition to kale and other brassicas.

Saving Seed

Say you notice a beautiful cabbage that suffered no frost damage, or some corn salad that is bigger and tastier than the rest. Are you simply going to pop them in the pot? How about letting them go to seed instead? Not only will saving your own seed save you money, but you will be propagating local strains of winter-hardy varieties that you can share with others. If the seed comes true every year you will have in hand a valuable resource.

Rob Johnston, of Johnny's Selected Seeds in Maine, has written a handy booklet, *Growing Garden Seeds* (see page 122), which will tell you most of what you need to know to save seeds correctly, and LD Hills has a verse in Chapter 8 of *Grow Your Own Fruits & Vegetables* which will help you learn how long each variety stays viable (see page 124).

The only caution I would make here is to say that when plants are going to seed they are frequently taller and bushier than when they are simply producing leaves and buds. It might be expedient to carefully transplant a winter variety to a separate part of your garden in February so that it won't interfere with your rotation scheme and take up all the room you had planned for spring lettuce, etc.

The True Seed Exchange, RFD 2, Princeton MO 64673, has Maritime Northwest members, and exchange with them might be valuable for you. It costs a dollar to join, which could end up saving you lots of money in the long run. You run your name in their newsletter, and state what you have extra seed of and what you would like to find.

Abundant Life Seed Foundation, Box 30018, Seattle WA 98103, will trade seeds, so if you have an excess you can call or write to see if they would like some of your variety. If you have already been saving seeds, and have valuable ones that either have been lost to the commercial market, or are an heirloom in your family, you should contact them, and Johnny's, for such things are important in our efforts to establish (reestablish?) a viable local agriculture.

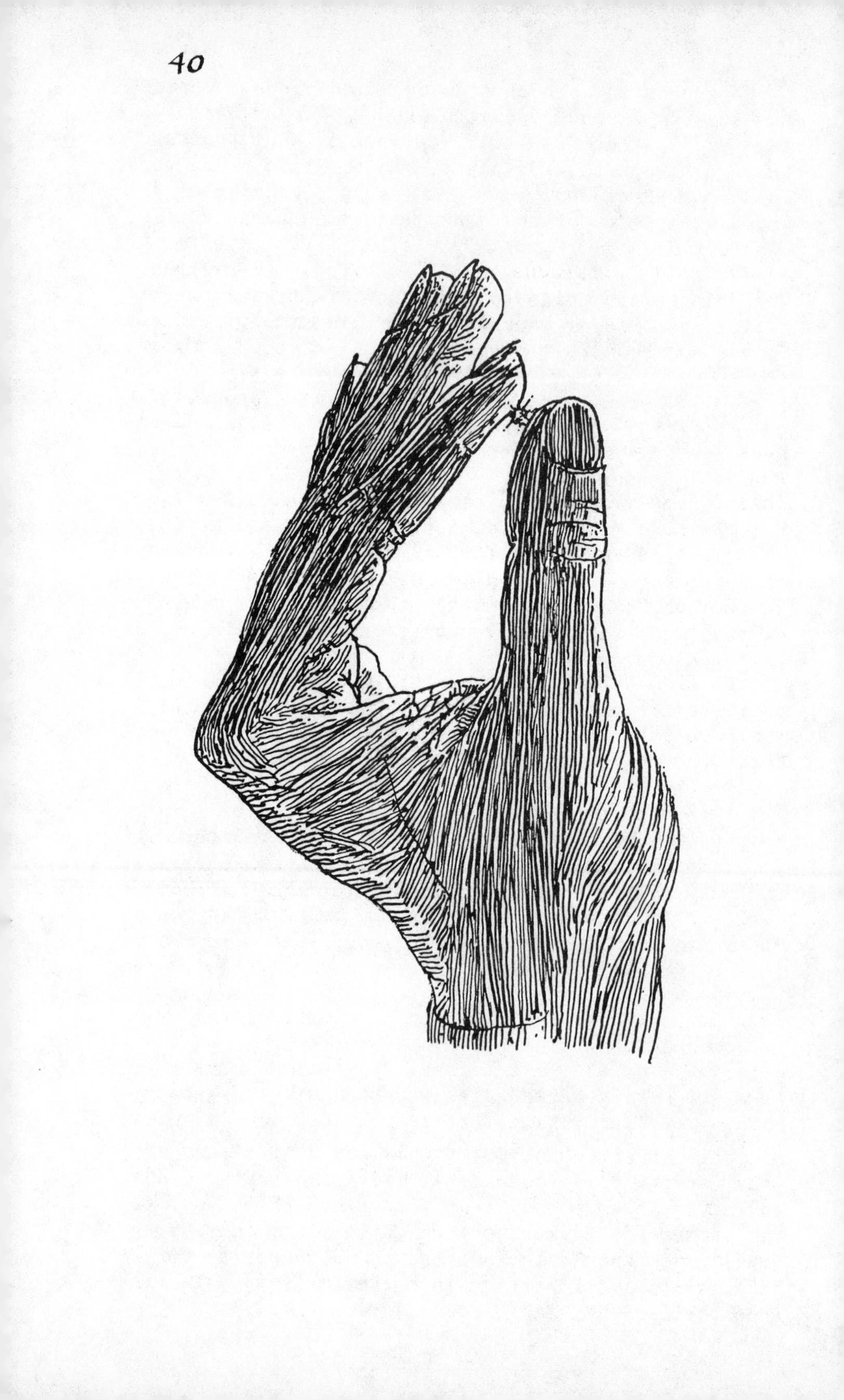

Self-Confidence

You might at first doubt that self-confidence could rate a place under Principles of Winter Gardening along with site, climate, or soil, but it certainly does. I became aware of this when I first started visiting other people's gardens. They would all spend the first few minutes apologizing for the terrible condition of their plot, excusing the state of the broccolis, pardoning the peas, and generally assuming that there must be something wrong with their garden.

Many had spent the day before weeding it as if I was their mother-in-law inspecting the dust on their mantel, assuming for some strange reason that I never had weeds in my garden, or that my broccolis never failed, nor my peas ever shriveled.

This made me feel bad, for I assume that the *first* principle of gardening is that it is an art devoted to the feeding of a family *by* that family, and that, while you may or may not appreciate the aesthetics of another's garden, if it feeds them then how it looks hardly matters.

You should have the self-confidence to do whatever is right for you. For example, you may have decided that Brussels sprouts are too much trouble, that *you* don't want to stand outside bent over in the rain for ten minutes cutting those tiny little knobs off the main stem and then spend an additional twenty minutes in the kitchen pruning and cleaning them before cooking; whereas in the same space you could have had a savoy cabbage, equally hardy, that you could have picked with one fell swoop of your knife, and devoted but three minutes to cutting up and sauteeing for dinner. But if your neighbor loves Brussels sprouts and hates savoys, who's to argue?

I don't think much of Rocket, but Judy loves it, so I included her rave review next to my phlegmatic one (see page 80) just to show you that you better have the self-confidence of your own palate, and to remind you that your garden is just as good as anyone's as long as it feeds you and you feed it back. And if you expect that, having written this book, I'm about to grow a model garden full of all the possibilities, well you're wrong. I will grow what I want to eat that year, nothing much else, and no doubt my carrots will still have rust fly and wireworm, and my mustards maggots.

Everything that I have tried to say here about the principles of winter gardening is to help give you a feeling for the parameters of getting crops off at low temperatures. I hope I have explained some things and given you a good overview of the problems. But written words don't give you the *experience*, and when it comes down to it, *your* experience in *your garden* is what counts the most.

Have faith in your own abilities, and in the plants, and just go ahead and experiment!

Footnotes

[1] Alther & Raymond, Improving Garden Soils with Green Manures.

[2] Pimental, "Food Production and the Energy Crisis," Science, Vol. 183.

[3] For example see Chan, Better Vegetable Gardens the Chinese Way.

[4] Philbrick & Gregg, Companion Plants.

[5] Pollard, Hooper & Moore, Hedges, p. 164. 1974. Taplinger Publications, New York.

[6] Mackenzie, Goat Husbandry, p. 149.

[7] Information on seaweed provided by Woody Deryckx.

Share Croppers

I haven't encountered too many pests or diseases during the actual winter. Slugs, mice, birds, and rot are the main exceptions. But for the slow plants, ones that have to grow all summer to produce in the winter, there are indeed some formidable sharecroppers. Take-alls might be a better term!

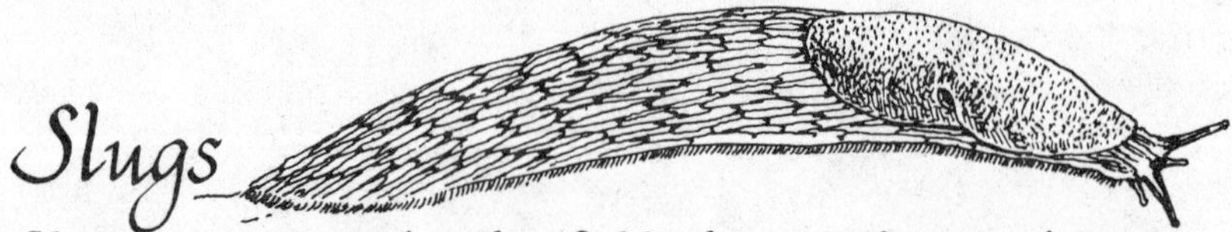

Slugs

Slugs are worst in the fall when you're trying to get the late plantings up and growing, and in the early spring when you're doing the same with the late spring crops.

Most varieties of slugs are scavengers and scroungers, prefering wilted, dying vegetation to young new stuff. The main reason they devastate your young seedlings is that there isn't much else 'round to eat, especially if you have bare plots of soil with a few tiny plants. There are, unfortunately, a few exceptions.

I found that in the city, where the especially omnivorous little imported grey English slugs abound in greater numbers than in the country, I could keep the predations down to a reasonable level by getting discarded outer cabbage and lettuce leaves at my local grocery, and spreading them down the rows or on the edges of the beds. At night I would go out with a flashlight and pick the slugs before bed. Same thing at dawn. During the day they hide under the leaves, so I got them that way also. But I suspect that even if you can't arrange to be so faithful it might not matter anyway.

An interesting pamphlet from the Henry Doubleday Research Associations (HDRA), *Slugs & the Gardener* (see page 127), indicates that you can catch slugs in your garden every night for a year and not make a dent in the population. These mollusks are migratory and you would have to organize your whole neighborhood into slug patrols. (Not a bad idea!)

Either that or change your community's ordinance about ducks. Ducks are very fond of slugs. They have a special technique of bill probing in grass and other low vegetation to ferret out low lying slugs that is very satisfying to watch. Ducks are also friendly, amusing, egg laying, good tasting and they fertilize rather than poison the environment.

In terms of the total picture, ducks don't consume much if any nonrenewable energy (none if you let the hens hatch out their own children), and so you are using one self-maintaining animal to control another. To my mind this is one of the best aspects of biological control, and I certainly advocate it whenever you are dealing with a "pest". It's a little harder with slugs than it is with some of the insects, but still an admirable goal.

If you have a small yard and your ducks show too much of a liking for your garden vegetables, try feeding them greens before you let them in the garden. If this doesn't work, then just use them to patrol the rest of the property, and you de-slug the garden. Ducks will still be worth it due to that migratory tendency of slugs.

However, if you have been using a chlorinated hydrocarbon (DDT family) on your property anywhere, I suggest you not eat the ducks or their eggs. Slugs are excellent concentrators of these poisons, and so they get into the ducks' fat (of which both they and the eggs have rather a lot).

Ducks, of course, are more suited to suburban and rural properties than they are to most city ones, so you might want to use some of the other forms of control if you are in such a situation.

Interestingly enough snakes are also slug predators, and hence are valuable in that regard, though they also consume toads which are another pest control. Probably the balance is in favor of the snakes, so leave them be.

Hedgehogs eat slugs too, but unfortunately they aren't native to this country. Maybe, if you are enterprising, you could rent one from a zoo.

One useful thing I discovered is to mulch low lying plants like lettuce with substances slugs don't like to hide under; wood shavings are good. Take care to avoid cedar. Hardwoods are best if you can get them.

A good side effect of this is that wood shavings have a drying effect that reduces rot. I never had any success with the stale-beer-in-a-cup method. Due to the rain, it seems that wouldn't be good in the cool times of the year anyhow.

A potentially practical organic bait solution for slugs is Fertosan Slug Destroyer. In spite of its name, it is herbal and only interferes with their copper metabolism and doesn't harm "worms, hedgehogs, birds or any other creature".[1] I am trying to find a US distributor. The British one is the Henry Doubleday Research Assoc., Bocking, Braintree, Essex, England. Write for price.

I guess I have to admit something: I *like* slugs. I think they are beautiful, useful as scavengers and have a right to live, especially the big black orange and spotted native ones. Their nature is to flow, albeit slowly, and I don't like to kill them. I'd rather pass that karma on to the ducks.

Rust Fly Maggot and Wireworm

Both rust fly maggots and wireworms attack carrots, the first mainly early in the season and the second later on. I lump them together because it is often hard for the gardener to tell which beastie it was that burrowed all through their carrots and left them tasting terrible and beginning to rot.

For attacks in the summer, raising the alkalinity with ashes in the soil has been reported as helpful. Apply along the row, every two weeks. In Europe, organic farmers lay green mosquito netting over the beds to protect them from the early layings of the fly.

For the later attacks, harvest the carrots as soon as they are mature, certainly by the end of September. If you put whole, untouched roots in damp sand or peat, they will store as well as in the ground, but not be bothered by these pests.

Cabbage Aphid

Cabbage aphids attack kale, cabbages, Brussels sprouts, etc. in the summer. The toxins from their feeding cause the leaves to warp and curl, and can stunt plants so badly they won't head up or produce when you want them to.

The aphids are parasitized by a minute wasp, however, whose offspring feed within the bodies of the aphids, turning them into little golden mummies. If you see a high proportion of mummies to feeding aphids, you can assume that control is underway. Then you only need to give the seedlings or plants a boost with manure teas or a mulch of partly aged horse manure.

If you can't find any predatory wasps (in a situation where pesticides have been used they could very well have been eliminated) and are in danger of losing your crop you can: 1) wipe the aphids off with your fingers, 2) spray with a very strong black tea with a bit of soap for wetting solution, or 3) spray with a soap (NOT detergent) solution. These are all last resort efforts, as you really don't want to mess up any biological balance that might still exist in your garden and neighborhood.

These aphids overwinter in the form of little black eggs on any of the cabbage tribe that you have growing, so in November or so you should spray with a nicotine solution made from old cigaret butts or pipe tobacco (careful—it's poisonous) to keep down the aphid population. Hopefully, you will also avoid killing the predatory wasps at this point. I don't know how they overwinter.

Other helpful predators are lacewings and lady beetles.

Cabbage Butterfly and Moth

I don't find the little green caterpillar larvae of the cabbage butterfly and moth to be much of a problem this side of the Cascades. I mention them because if I don't I'll get a bunch of complaints from folk who do have problems. They can both be knocked out with Thuricide, or any other *Bacillus thuringensis* preparation, which is specific to butterfly and moth larvae. As with most pests, you should only treat for them if you have a *real* problem—a real problem meaning you could lose a crop you can't replace, not that you have a few stray caterpillars on a well-developed plant. You might not be able to sell a cabbage with a few holes in it, but you sure can *eat* one.

Cabbage Root Fly Maggot

The cabbage root fly maggot is a *real* impediment to the year-round gardener, as the crucifers, which they attack, represent some of the hardiest and best of the winter crops.

The fly, about the size of a small house fly, lays its eggs in the earth right by the stem of seedling or transplanted crucifers (cabbage, broccoli, cauliflower, radish, turnip, kohlrabi, rutabaga, mustard and collards). These eggs hatch into maggots which burrow to the stem and roots of young crucifer plants.

The maggots eat the stem and roots, sometimes killing the plants outright, but more often merely stunting them. The plants will look small, but normal, to the inexperienced gardener, but then during a sunny dry spell they will all of a sudden wilt and keel over. If you then dig up the plants you will find the little white maggots have almost totally destroyed the roots and stem, and the plants have just been sitting in the soil.

If it is a wet year, the plants sometimes manage to send out new roots from the stem above the area that has been damaged. However, if your plants have been too badly set back, they won't produce a head (or whatever they're supposed to do), and it's best to delegate them to the compost heap and put something else in their place.

Prevention is by far the best strategy against the root fly maggot and the first element of prevention is to be aware of the laying cycle of the fly.[2]

The idea behind the chart on the following page is to plan sowing and transplanting so that you can get your plants settled into their permanent homes between egg laying peaks. Hopefully, they will then be tough enough to withstand the maggots. After a certain point of maturity the maggots are no longer as likely to kill or stunt the plant.

Root Fly Egg Laying Cycle

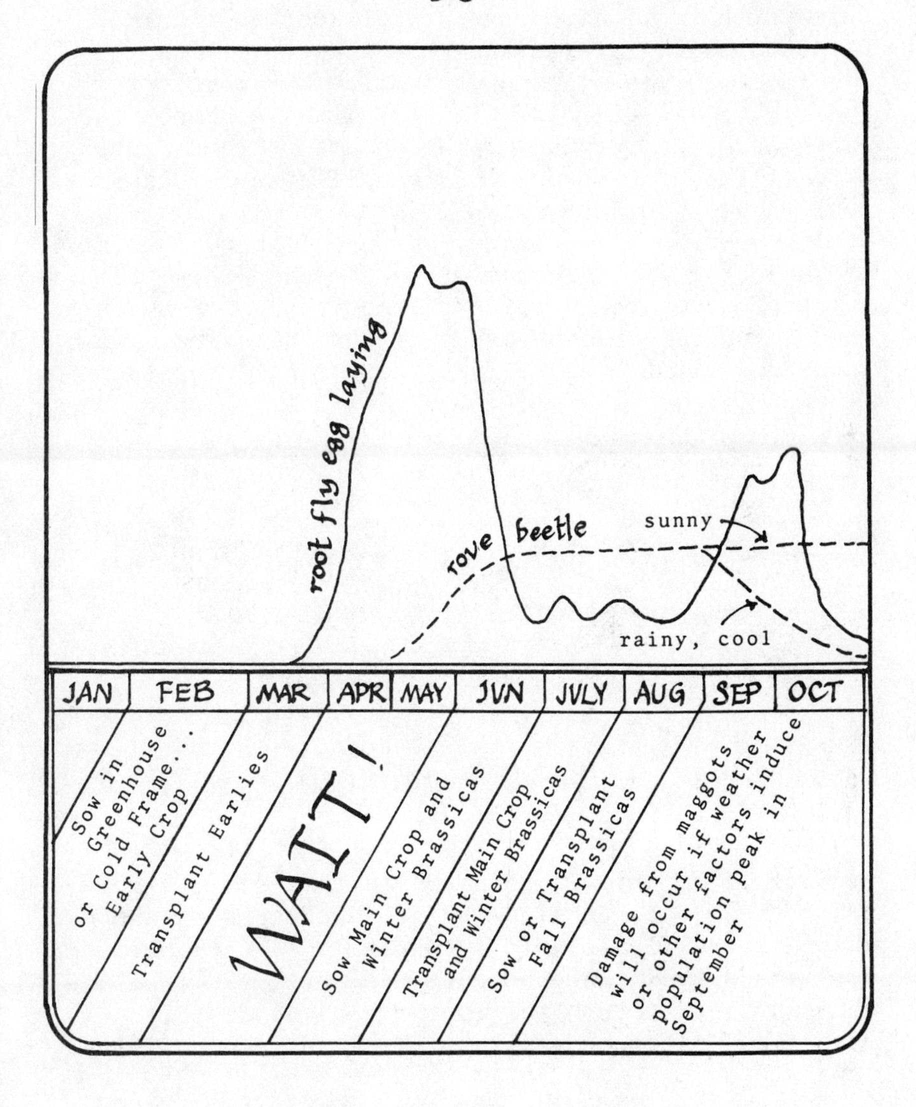

Key

———	Root Fly Maggot
- - - -	Rove & Ground Beetle

You can get off a large percentage of your cole crops by this method of timing your planting. You want to get your seed or transplants in the ground as soon as possible to give them the time they need to mature and to get a good crop of brassicas. To do this you have to have some way of keeping track of when the laying starts and when it stops.

Sometimes you will see the flies but more often you won't. What I did this spring was to check the earth each week around the stems after transplanting a small amount of broccolis (cauliflowers or cabbages would have done just as well).

If you transplant properly—that is bury them at or above the first leaves or cotyledons—then there is a lot of stem area before the root zone. When you check, you carefully brush away the soil from around the stem. If the eggs are there you will see them, a

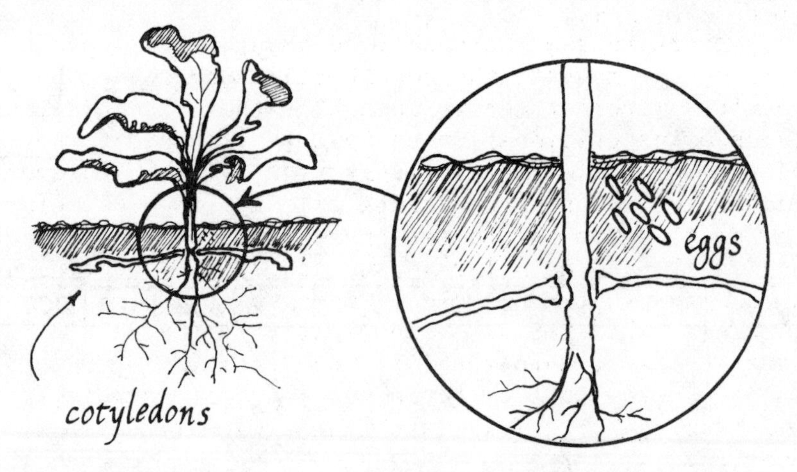

small mass of white cocoon-shaped things. I simply pinch these out, putting the soil and eggs on the path where they will die. In my experience, they have only been a short distance beneath the soil, and it isn't necessary to disturb the roots when you do this. I fertilized afterwards with fish or seaweed emulsion anyhow.

This method is a lot of work, but I feel that checking for eggs is better than many other strategies for dealing with the root fly maggot. The method is more effective than, for example, tar paper collars and less awkward than plastic cartons. Checking for eggs gives you information about whether or not the fly in fact *is* laying.

If you only have a very small area to grow your food in, and are set on having winter broccolis and cauliflowers, then every plant counts. You could go to the trouble of using a screened frame to place over your seedlings and young transplants till the danger period is over. This technique has been used by the Farallones folk, and has been reported in the Olkowski's book, *The City People Book of Raising Food* (see page 125). You must, of course, then make as sure as possible that there are no pupae in the soil to emerge, mate, and lay eggs.

This screen technique might work in areas, such as Seattle's 85th St. P Patch, where extensive cultivation of cole crops has been going on for many years, populations of the fly have built up, laying happens continuously, and it seems almost impossible to get plants through undamaged from any sowing. Winter Garden Project participants in the P Patch reported that in the rainy summer of '76 they lost most of their cole crops.*

In part this was probably because the main predators of the maggot, the rove beetles and the ground beetles, were not active enough, either from previously used insecticides, or because of the cold. The beetles need a warmer soil than the flies do to emerge and be active, so the maggots will get to work before the beetles are out to eat them. The roves are black and quick, and both larvae and adults lack the long hard wings that are typical of most beetles. Sometimes when you are transplanting you will see them, scurrying away into the soil and debris. You may find damage on the root of the plant, but not maggots, and then you can be fairly sure that they were eaten by beetles.

The maggots may have escaped and pupated too. You can find these little brown forms resting in the soil when you are digging over a cabbage bed or row in the early spring, and you should destroy them. The birds will help you on this if you let the turned up soil sit a day or so, and the adult beetles will eat them later in the summer.

Many people have reported success with one strategy or another for dealing with the root fly maggot, but often these successes haven't been duplicated by other gardeners. I suspect that some of the successful

---

* Dar Rundberg of Seattle has suggested that *no* brassicas be grown at the 85th St. P Patch site for enough time to reduce the root fly population.

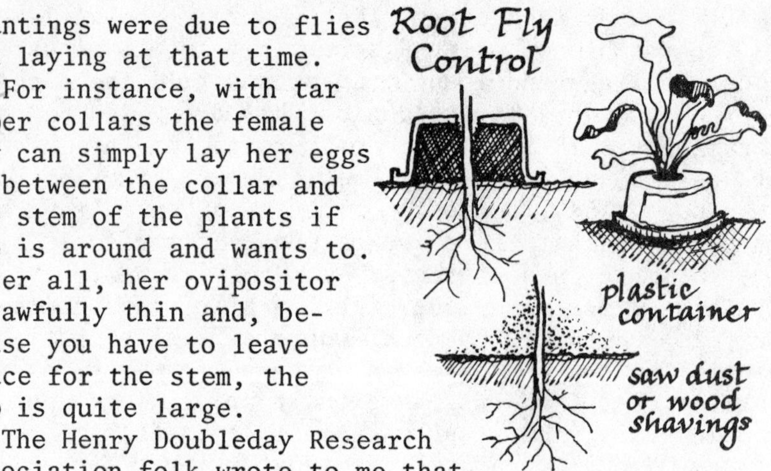

plantings were due to flies not laying at that time.

For instance, with tar paper collars the female fly can simply lay her eggs in between the collar and the stem of the plants if she is around and wants to. After all, her ovipositor is awfully thin and, because you have to leave space for the stem, the gap is quite large.

The Henry Doubleday Research Association folk wrote to me that they had success by creating a dark space that the fly wouldn't lay in with plastic cottage cheese cartons around the base of the plants.

Wood ashes *may* also work against the root fly maggot. Elaine Davenport, one of the founders of the Tilth Association, says that Black people in Alabama have used ashes for generations when growing collards to get them past the critical fly laying point. They put a handful of ashes in the soil with each transplant, and then sprinkle more over the top of the soil. I would think the alkalinity might burn the tender seedlings but apparently it doesn't.

One commercial grower in the Winter Garden Project, Gary Franco on Lopez Island, was successful this year ('77) in carrying off an early crop of organic Snowball cauliflower, and Early Jersey Wakefield and Golden Acre cabbage with a very thick mulch of sawdust. He sowed these varieties in March and transplanted them out in late April and May. He then mulched them with the sawdust. He lost at most 5 percent of the plants. The previous year in the same field he lost 85 percent of the crop. This, of course, was an experiment without a control.

I've read that European growers sow early cabbages and broccolis in cold frames in the fall (late August/ September) and overwinter them. In February, when severe frosts are no longer likely, they plant them out in their permanent location. They are then large enough to withstand maggot damage by the time egg laying starts.

Most of the methods of control I've mentioned, except mulching and timing your crops to avoid the main laying, are too laborious to practice on a commercial scale. Commercial cole crop growers around here use a poison called Diazenon, which they put in the soil. Hopefully someone will soon develop other biological techniques so that early crops of brassicas can be planted commercially without poisons.

Local organic growers should try mulching, over-wintering, and any other methods that can be thought up for successfully growing early brassica crops. The extra profit might make the extra effort worth it, and it would help reintroduce fresh organic produce to the local markets, coops, and restaurants of the area.

Checking Your Results

Before we can jump to conclusions about any method of deterring root fly maggots, many gardeners and farmers will have to try the method next to unprotected brassicas to see the comparison.

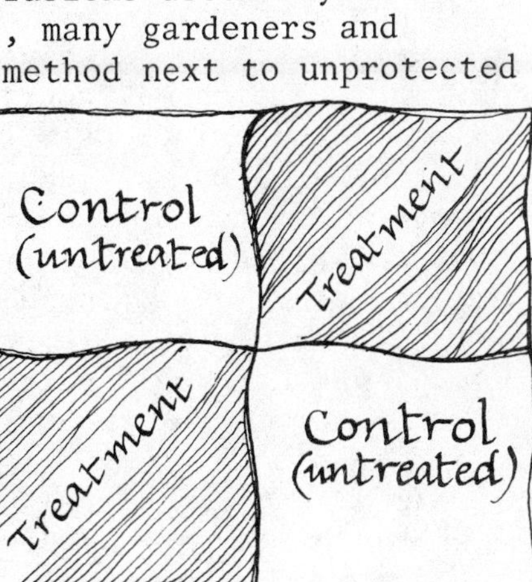

To check your results, use control sections in your next cabbage or early broccoli bed. Divide the bed into quarters as in the chart on the right. Then treat the shaded areas with whatever technique you choose, leaving the open areas as controls.

If you can, check for the amount of egg laying activity, as well as checking for plant damage and unharvestable plants. General health and appearance of the plants, presence or absence of other pests, size and taste of harvest, and duration of harvest would be other differences to observe. Record your results, and let us know what you discover.

Footnotes

[1] Hills, Growing Your Own Fruits & Vegetables, p. 86.

[2] Information on root fly maggots and other insect pests provided by Woody Deryckx, The Evergreen State College, Olympia WA 98505.

Which Vegetables and Herbs to Grow

january king

Introduction

I've tried to make the Vegetable List as comprehensive as possible so that you will be exposed to the full range of vegetables suitable for cool season cropping. I don't suggest you grow all of them, however, or even most of them in your first year. I haven't grown all of them myself, and say when information comes from other folk or from books.

In most instances, I don't give general cultural requirements for each plant unless it's important. As I am trying to keep this book as short as possible, you' can find cultural information in the other books I have recommended, especially AJ Simons' *New Vegetable Grower's Handbook*, and LD Hill's *Grow Your Own Fruits & Vegetables*.

Nomenclature

The term "sow" is used to refer to putting seed in the ground (or pot, flat, etc.). The term "plant" refers to putting a plant in the ground (transplanting).

I separated out the *Cruciferae* to begin the Vegetable List to make that group clear as a unit to you.

I experienced difficulty finding Latin names for some varieties, as many garden books and seed catalogues don't routinely list them. I did the best I could, though there probably are a few errors.

For taxonomy I referred to:

Oxford Book of Food Plants, Harrison, Masefield, Wallis. 1969. Oxford University Press.

Wild Flowers of Britain & Northern Europe. 1974.

Grow Your Own Fruits & Vegetables, LD Hills. 1975. Faber & Faber, London.

The Tsang & Ma International Catalogue. 1977. California.

Flora of the Pacific Northwest. C Leo Hitchcock and Arthur Cronquist. 1973. University of Washington Press, Seattle.

Seeds

Nowadays commercial seed companies are involved with selling as much as possible to largely inexperienced gardeners and will often list all sorts of "new" varieties that only last in the catalogues a few years. In the process, many old varieties suitable for local conditions and special purposes (such as winter hardiness) have lost out. Under Sources, page 121, I have given the addresses of as many seed companies as I could locate that still carry these varieties, but there is no telling if and when they may be discontinued. If you find that a vegetable or a vegetable variety that I have mentioned is no longer carried, you can either try to replace it with a similar one, try to convince the company to carry it again, or start on your own treasure hunt to turn up someone who has the seed. Many good gardeners save their own seed; advertising through coop newsletters, The True Seed Exchange, or gardening societies might help you locate them.

Seed Source Abbreviations

(ABL)	Abundant Life
(A&B)	Alexander & Brown
(DAM)	William Dam
(H&H)	Herbs & Honey (Nancy Fisher)
(JSS)	Johnny's Selected Seeds
(MB)	Meadowbrook Herb Garden
(SGC)	Seattle Garden Center
(STK)	Stokes
(TIL)	Tillinghast
(T&M)	Thompson & Morgan
(T&MI)	Tsang & Ma International

Hardiness

I have used the designations Very Hardy, Hardy and Half Hardy. Very Hardy are plants such as leeks, salsify, and corn salad that may live through temperatures as low as zero degrees Fahrenheit. Hardy are plants such as kale, cabbages, and onions that will mostly go through frosts of ten degrees Fahrenheit. Half Hardy are those plants that die at freezing or a little below (18°F at the most). These designations are for the purposes of this book only; most of the plants mentioned are hardy compared to other garden vegetables. All freeze-out data is from max/min thermometers used in Winter Garden Project except where noted.

Cloches

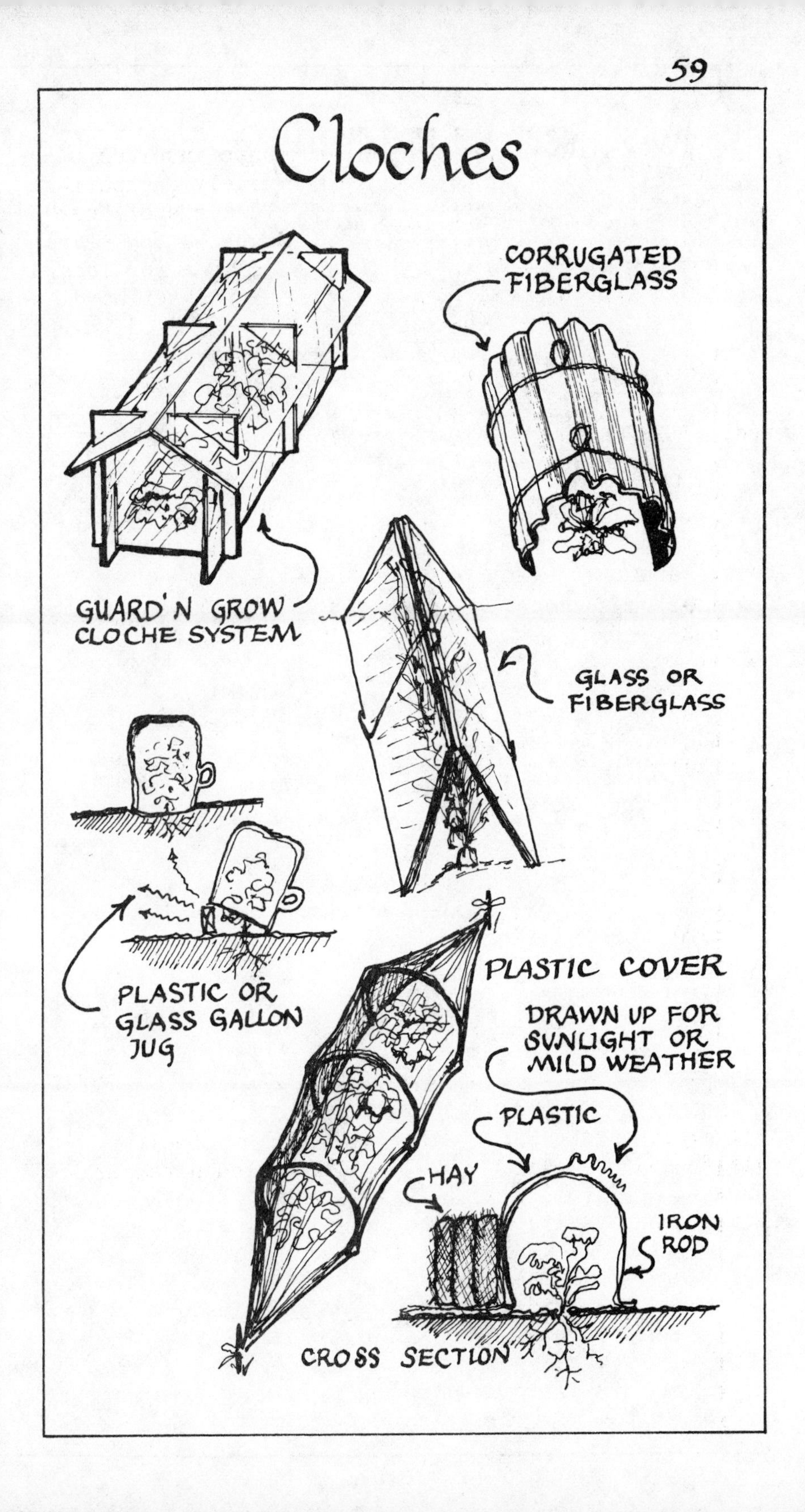
CORRUGATED FIBERGLASS
GUARD'N GROW CLOCHE SYSTEM
GLASS OR FIBERGLASS
PLASTIC OR GLASS GALLON JUG
PLASTIC COVER
DRAWN UP FOR SUNLIGHT OR MILD WEATHER
PLASTIC
HAY
IRON ROD
CROSS SECTION

Winter Gardening Calendar

In using the Winter Gardening Calendar, remember that sowing dates may differ depending on site, season, and crop variety.

Successions of quick crops, such as lettuce, rocket, etc. are best sown about a month apart.

Sowing dates *are based on the Seattle area.* Freeze out *temperatures are based on Winter Garden Project observations, 1975-1977.*

The calendar omits most food planted for harvest between June and September.

SOWING DATES	HARVEST	FREEZE OUT (*=may go lower)
January		
EARLY		
Cress (sow in darkened cold frame)	10 days	
MID (in hot frame or hot shed)		
Beets/Carrots/Lettuce/Onion Sets/Radishes	March-June	
LATE		
Fava Beans (if weather permits)	May-June	
February		
EARLY		
Turnips	March-April	
Fava Beans	May-June	
MID		
GREENHOUSE/COLD FRAME (for transplanting)		
Parsley	July-April	9°F
Leeks	Sept-March	9°F*
Broccoli, Italian Green Sprouting	June	18°F
Broccoli, Nine Star Perennial	Nov-on	9°F
Brussels Sprouts, Tall	Dec-March	9°F*
Celery/Celeriac	March	18°F
OUTDOORS		
Turnips	March-April	
Rocket	April	
March		
EARLY		
Brussels Sprouts	Dec-March	9°F
MID		
Red Cabbage	Aug-Sept	
Rocket	April-May	
LATE—SPRING EQUINOX		
Lettuce (if you missed before)	April-May	
Leeks (if you missed before)-outside	Sept-April	9°F
Parsley (if you missed before)	Oct-March	9°F*
Parsnips	Oct-March	0°F?
Burdock	Nov-April	0°F
Salsify/Scorzonera	Nov-April	0°F
Chicory Root, for forcing	Jan-March	
April/May		
Sow same crops as above. If you live much south of Seattle, you might try moving some June plantings here.		
June		
EARLY		
Last date for most winter cropping roots listed above	Sept-Dec	
Cabbage—fall & winter varieties	see pages 70-71	
Cauliflower	see pages 70-71	
Brussels Sprouts, Dwarf	Sept-Dec	15°F
Broccoli, Purple Sprouting	Dec-March	10°F?
Broccoli, St. Valentine	Feb-March	15°F

Sowing Dates	Harvest	Freeze Out
JUNE		
LATE—SUMMER SOLSTICE	Sept-on	18 F
Broccoli—Italian Green Sprouting,	Sept-on	
Purple Sprouting	Sept-March	
Endive/Escarole	Sept-on	10° F*
Beets—Lutz, Sugar, Winterkeeper	Oct-March	15°F
Kale (for transplanting)	Oct-March	0°F*
July		
EARLY		
Rutabaga	Sept-Nov	?
Florence Fennel (till mid-July)	Oct-heavy frost	18°F
Broccoli, Italian Green Sprouting	Nov-Dec	15°F
MID		
Beans—Bush/Pole	Sept-frost	30°F
Peas (60 day varieties)	Sept-frost	30°F?
Kohlrabi	Sept-Jan	25°F
Beets—small varieties (e.g., Detroit)	Sept-March	
Lutz		30°F
Swiss Chard	Sept-March	10°F
Broccoli—fast varieties, Chinese Broccoli, Green Comet, Waltham, Italian Green Sprouting	Sept-March	18°F
Chervil	Oct-May	
Chinese Cabbage	Oct-Nov	
Collards	Oct-Nov	20°F
Kale (nontransplanting varieties)	Oct-May	
Turnips	Nov-Jan	10°F
Spinach	Sept-Dec	?
LATE		
Onions, early bulb types	May	10°F
Endive/Escarole	Sept-on	
Radishes, oriental	Sept-frost	10°F
Spinach	Sept-Nov	?
Swiss Chard	Sept-March	10°F
August		
EARLY		
Chinese Cabbage	Sept	18°F
Turnips	Sept-Jan	10°F?
Raab	Feb-March	?
MID		
Onions, bunching for greens	March-June	10°F
Onions, early bulb types	May	10°F
Rocket	Sept-on	?
Lettuce	Sept-Jan	18°F
Mustards—Tai Tsai, Mizuna, Bok Choy etc.	Sept-April	18°F
Corn Salad	Oct-April	0°F
Spinach	Oct-April	9°F
Broccoli, Italian Green Sprouting	Feb-on	15°F
Winter Cress	all winter	?
LATE		
Cabbages—April, Hisipi, Jersey Wakefield	March-April	18°F
Carrot—Frubund	April	15°F?
Radishes	Sept-Jan	18°F
September		
Cabbages—April, Hisipi, Jersey Wakefield	April-May	
Onion Sets, for greens	Oct-May	10°F
Spinach	Nov-May	0°F
Corn Salad (warm microclimate only)	Nov-May	0°F
Lettuce (in cold frames or greenhouse)	Dec-May	18°F
October/November		
Fava Beans, Long Pod	May-June	?
Peas	May-June	?
Jerusalem Artichokes	frost-April	0°F*
Chickweed	Sept-June	0°F*
Garlic, Onion Sets, Shallots	Nov/Dec-April	10°F

typical
crucifer
flower

Vegetable List

CRUCIFERS

The *Cruciferae* group is so large and important to the year-round gardener that it merits its own section. Included in the group are *Brassica oleracea* (cabbages, broccolis, cauliflowers, and some kales), *Brassica pekinensis* (Pe-Tsai, Nappa, Chihili), *Brassica chinesis* (Bok Choy or Pak-Choi), *Brassica rapa* (turnip and some kales), and *Brassica napus* (rutabaga). Then there are the closely related radishes (*Raphanes sativus*), horseradish (*Amoracia rusticana*), rocket (*Eruca sativa*), cress (*Lapidium sativum*), watercress (*Nasturtiun officionale*), and winter or American cress (*Barbarea verna*).

I list these not to overwhelm you, bore you, or impress you, but because they form a horticultural group. They have similar needs and diseases and they have similar effects on the soil. When you practice a rotation, with a few exceptions, they should be considered as a group and *rotated together*.

The exceptions are watercress, which belongs in water or moist soil, horseradish, and winter cress which can go in permanent herb beds.

Our most important brassicas evolved in Northwest Europe, in the maritime climate there. Hence, they are adaptable to *our* maritime climate, and have special pertinence to this region.

There are many different varieties that have been bred over the centuries in Europe to crop at different times of the year. This can best be illustrated by perusing a page from the British seed catalogue of Thompson & Morgan, or the Scottish one of Alexander & Brown (see pages 121-122). Most of these old varieties (or the newer ones derived from them) are SLOW maturing, taking as long as ten months in the ground.

The newer varieties (many of which were developed in North America to adapt to the stress of a continental climate) are FAST maturing and, if planted in the spring, will head up before the snow flies and the deep killing frosts set in. These newer varieties are the ones most featured in the US and Canadian catalogues. While they do well here in the Northwest, they don't take full advantage of our long cool growing seasons compared to European varieties such as: January King cabbage, Autumn Veitch Giant cauliflower, or Purple Sprouting broccoli.

There are also the small pointed-head types, (the Wakefields, Greyhound, Hispi, and April) which, with good culture, will head up in the early spring from an autumn sowing. These can also be sown in February for a quick loose cabbage in June and July. This, in fact, is how they are mostly used today. Few people realize they were originally developed to stand through the winter in a maritime environment.

Basically, most of the European brassicas are heavy nitrogen feeders, need lime, and are susceptible to attack by club root, cabbage moth and butterfly, cabbage root fly, and grey aphid. Most benefit from transplanting as it aids their root system. For individual preferences and cultural tips read Hills, Simons, and Sherwell-Cooper (see pages 124,126).

Oriental brassicas also do well here but it's harder to find cultural information on them. Both Hills and Simons have some suggestions, as well as Tsang & Ma and Johnny's Seeds catalogues. Chan's book (see page 124) is also helpful on some types.

Broccoli

Brassica oleracea Hardy

Italian Green Sprouting (ABL,TIL)
Nine Star Perennial (T&M,A&B)
Purple Sprouting (A&B,T&M,ABL-as cauliflower)
St. Valentine (TIL)

There is some confusion in the literature about what exactly the difference is between the cauliflowers and the broccolis because the names have been used interchangeably on the market. *The Oxford Book of Food Plants* has the most illuminating discussion on the matter, though too brief. *Cole Crops* by Neuhof is also interesting if you care to read about this subject in those rainy winter hours (see Books You Should Read, page 124).

Color (contrary to most US consumers' and gardeners' experiences) is not the diagnostic characteristic. "Broccolis" come in white, purple, and green and usually, though not always, are *sprouters*. Cauliflowers of the white sort that we know in this country (Early Snowball, etc.) are more likely to produce just one central head and then no more. There are seed companies, however, which carry green and purple "cauliflowers" that sprout, so I suspect it's mostly a nomenclature problem as the two are after all the same species.

Herein I will follow the seed catalogues' usage (with comments), not because I think them accurate, but because whatever the horticultural origin, you must look for them and purchase them by the name the seed companies choose to use. What was a broccoli in 1900 may now be called a cauliflower, and what is a broccoli in a British catalogue may be a cauliflower in North America.

Italian Green Sprouting (ABL,TIL)

A "cut and come again" type, Italian Green Sprouting is a standard variety, and was the most successful broccoli that I tried in Seattle. I sowed it from February (in the greenhouse) till August (outdoors) and had it cropping year-round. The July sowings produced till December and the August ones from late February on. Some plants lasted longer than others, almost a full year, making many little sprouts in the spring.

Italian Green Sprouting is the hardiest of the green broccolis (but not of the white; e.g., Nine Star Perennial). It freezes out around 15°F, especially after a rainy summer when it has put on a lot of soft growth. A simple cloche arrangement will help it through wet or much colder weather.

Nine Star Perennial (A&B,T&M)

One of the more unusual broccolis, Nine Star Perennial is a white sprouter. If sown in June and July it just puts on leafy growth in the first year, then sends out small heads from March onward.

I suspect that by sowing in February in a cold frame and moving out as soon as possible, one might get a late summer or midwinter crop. I did have several plants live through 9°F, so it's the hardiest one I know of at the moment, and fairly good for the foothills. It takes up a lot of space, however, needs a rich soil to begin with, and side dressings of compost to keep on producing. It's susceptible to grey aphid, so spray in the late fall with nicotine solution.

Purple Sprouting (ABL, A&B, T&M)

Listed in the British catalogues for overwintering. My Seattle trials of these from American seed were poor, but I'm trying the Thompson & Morgan seed again this winter because I feel it's worth experimenting with and worth trying to get a hardy local variety. Sow in June/July.

St. Valentine (TIL)

A slow grower, St. Valentine broccoli needs to be sown in June and transplanted in July to produce in February/March, unless you garden is in a warm area or south of Seattle. It isn't hardy below 15°F, so you need to put it under protection if you get deeper frosts. It is white and tight-headed like cauliflower.

The cultural requirements of broccolis are well known to most gardeners, so the only special comment I have regarding growing them in the winter is that, due to the nature of their flowers, they are susceptible to rot.

If you live in an area of high rainfall (over 45 inches), think about sheltering them from the rain. The simplest way of doing this is to spread one of the big leaves over the smaller leaves, florets, and the main stem. This latter is important because once you have cut the main stem, it too will start to rot. If you slice it on an angle, there is less chance of rain collecting on the stem and rotting the whole core of the plant.

Brussels Sprouts

B. *oleracea va gemifera* Very Hardy

Cambridge (T&M)
Catskill (ABL)
Citadel (T&M,A&B)
Early Dwarf Danish (JSS)

Brussels sprouts, along with leeks and kale, are the *sine qua non* of winter hardy vegetables. They are available from November (Early Dwarf Danish) till March (Citadel, Cambridge, Catskill), and in April you can eat the sprouts as they start to flower and taste

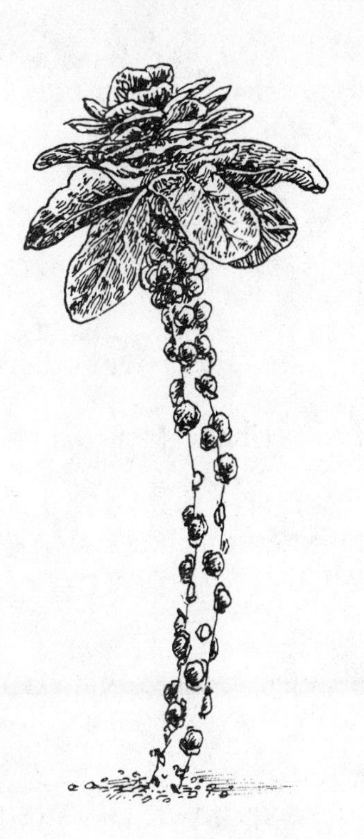

much like broccoli.

The tall Brussels sprouts, Cambridge, Catskill, and Citadel, can be exceptionally hardy. Use these European types for your late winter crops.

Some of the dwarf varieties (Early Dwarf Danish, et al.) were selected for heavy early crops. They will produce early in the fall, but will not stand in good condition beyond December in colder areas.

For awhile I thought my tall Brussels sprouts weren't doing well because I had only seen pictures of dwarf varieties which have the sprouts growing jam packed against each other. The tall varieties, however, have sprouts widely spaced, which means they don't rot as easily in midwinter The sprouts on the tall varieties are also smaller, more dense, and they keep better.

The tall varieties need a long season to develop a good root system and height before they put on sprouts, so it's best to start them in February or early March. If you don't have a greenhouse, a cold frame will do fine.

Transplant in March or early April at about 3-in. high. I have read they are more resistant to root fly maggot than the other brassicas, and I have found some indication that this is so. However, you can mulch them deeply with sawdust or check them periodically for eggs if it seems warranted in your site.

The late varieties,and plants that don't get enough sun, tend to get tall and need staking in July to support them. Other than that, they only need weeding till September.

Start picking sprouts from the bottom and, in the fall, break the bottom leaves off the plants. Don't leave any lower leaves or sprouts (even if they're not edible) to avoid rot. When you are all done with the sprouts, you can take the tops of the plants too; they're delicious.

If you have lots of sprouts and don't get around to picking them till March, they will start to flower on you. Don't leave them. They are still good in stir-fries. In fact, I think Brussels sprouts are better sauteed than steamed.

Cabbage

B. oleracea — Hardy to Very Hardy

MID-WINTER GREENS

Christmas Drumhead-January King-Winter Monarch (T&M,A&B)

REDS

Langediker Winter Keeper (DAM)-Mammoth Red Rock (STK,DAM)-Meteor (STK)-Red Danish (STK)

SAVOYS

Drumhead (A&B)-Ice Queen (DAM)-Netted Savoy (TIL)
Omskirk (A&B)-Savoy King (T&M)-Winterking (DAM)

EARLY SPRING

April (T&M,A&B)-Durham Early (A&B)-Greyhound (T&M)
Hispi (T&M)-Jersey Wakefield (ABL,TIL,SGC)

MID-WINTER GREENS

It is theoretically possible to have cabbage producing in your garden most of the year if you match variety with planting dates. A chart follows which shows you which kinds I've tried and which ones are being tried at Pragtree Farm this year.

Of these, January King and the savoys came through the winter with minimal damage, and tasted as good in March as they did in November.

REDS

Though they come in early, many individual red cabbages stood through the heaviest frosts. Sometimes they would get a bit crummy—slimy actually!—on the outside, but as long as the core didn't freeze they stood all right and the inside tasted fine.

SAVOYS

These cabbages are not well known in America. Savoys are loose open cabbages and don't have a very long shelf life, probably a strong contributing factor to their lack of popularity. But they taste wonderful,

winter monarch

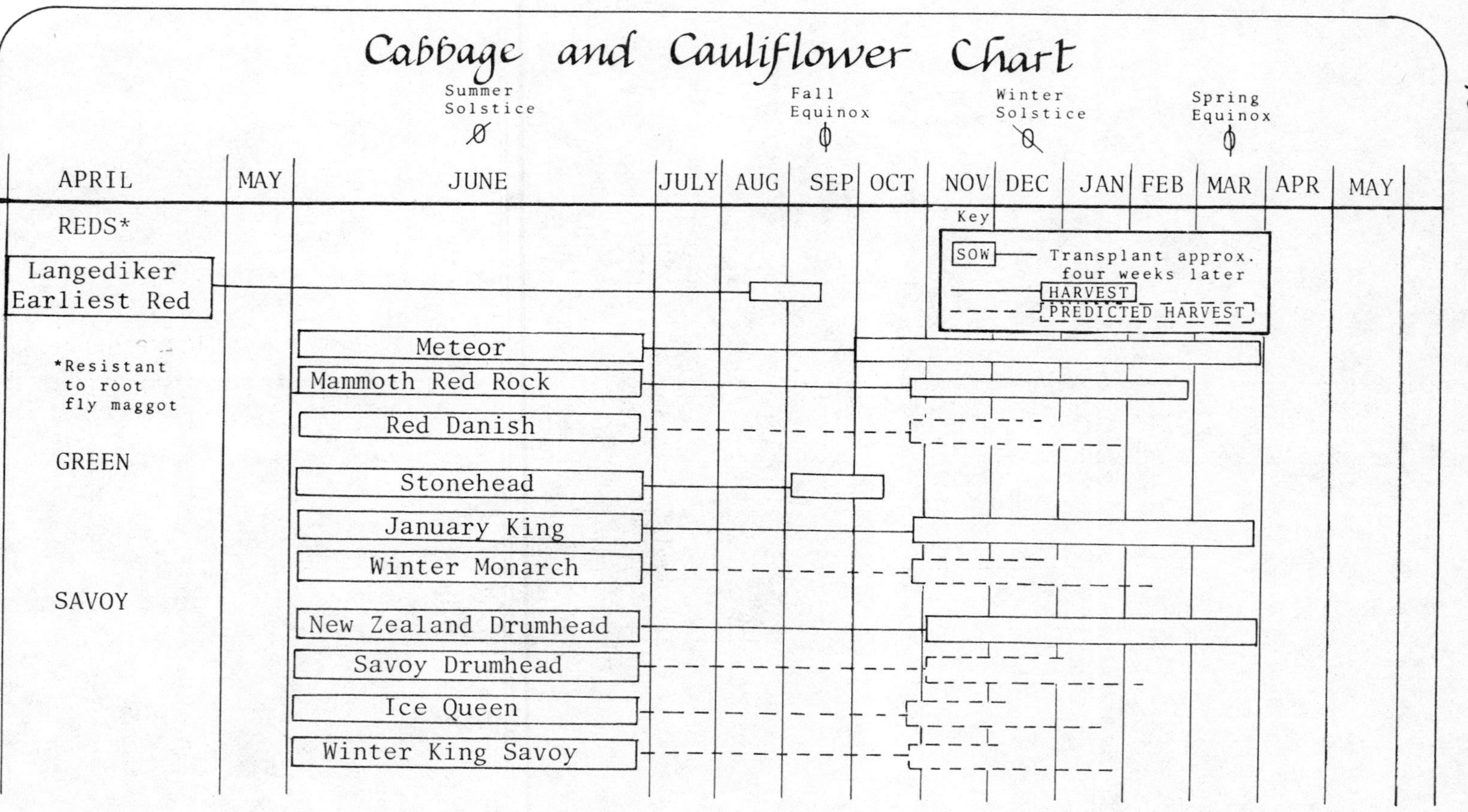
Cabbage and Cauliflower Chart
Summer Solstice
Fall Equinox
Winter Solstice
Spring Equinox
APRIL
MAY
JUNE
JULY
AUG
SEP
OCT
NOV
DEC
JAN
FEB
MAR
APR
MAY
REDS*
Langediker Earliest Red
*Resistant to root fly maggot
Meteor
Mammoth Red Rock
Red Danish
GREEN
Stonehead
January King
Winter Monarch
SAVOY
New Zealand Drumhead
Savoy Drumhead
Ice Queen
Winter King Savoy
Key
SOW
Transplant approx. four weeks later
HARVEST
PREDICTED HARVEST

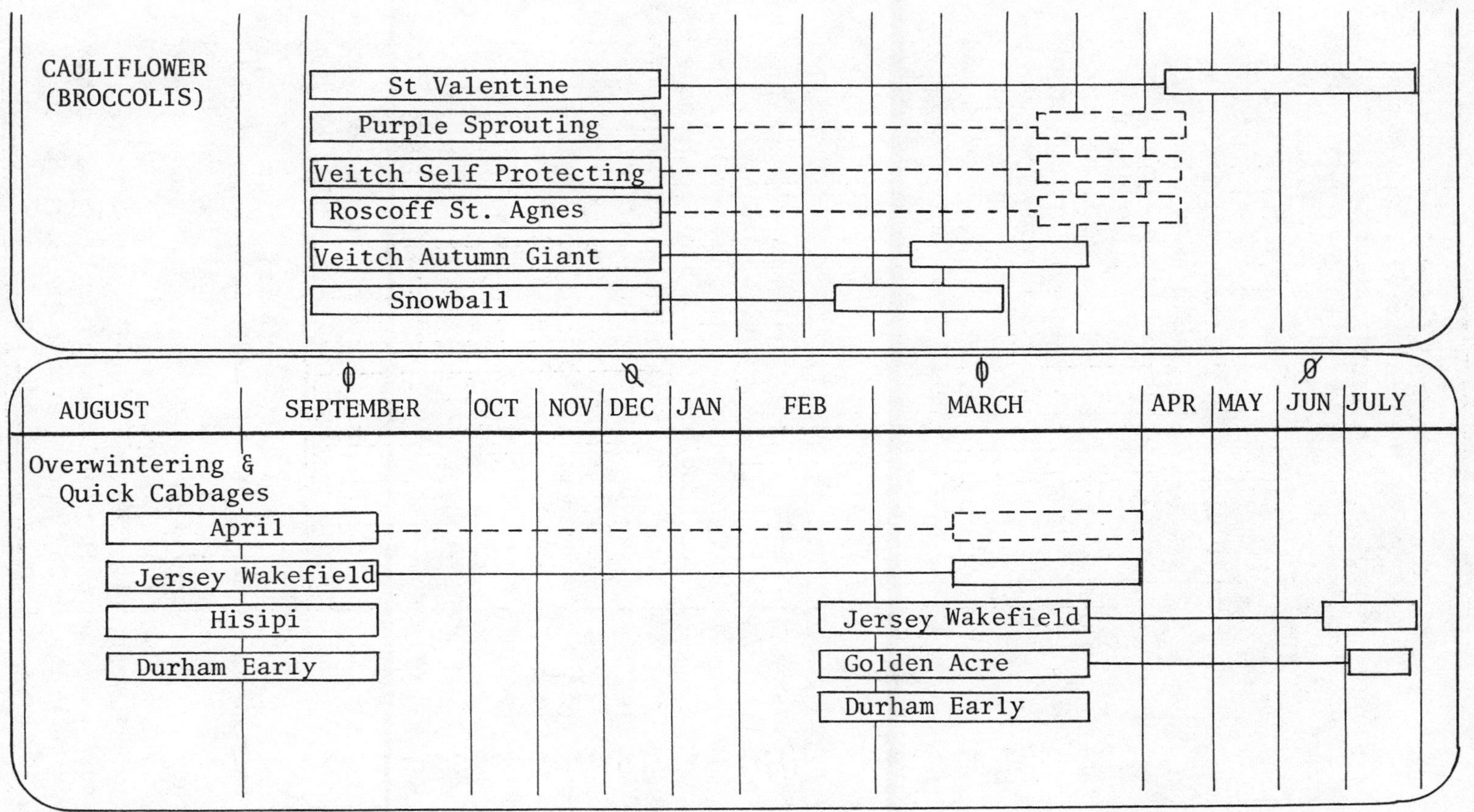
CAULIFLOWER
(BROCCOLIS)
St Valentine
Purple Sprouting
Veitch Self Protecting
Roscoff St. Agnes
Veitch Autumn Giant
Snowball
AUGUST
SEPTEMBER
OCT
NOV
DEC
JAN
FEB
MARCH
APR
MAY
JUN
JULY
Overwintering &
Quick Cabbages
April
Jersey Wakefield
Hisipi
Durham Early
Jersey Wakefield
Golden Acre
Durham Early

ice queen savoy

have more greenness to the head than other cabbages and are certainly worthy of attention by the winter gardener and cook. They are also very beautiful. The old varieties are the hardiest of the cabbages and stand well in the rain.

Their name comes from an area in northwestern Italy, and is also used as an adjective to describe the intense crinkling of their leaves. This is thought to impart some extra hardiness to plants that have it (e.g., Cold Resistant Savoy spinach).

EARLY SPRING

For spring in milder areas, or under cloches in the foothills, there are Jersey Wakefield and April. My second year winter gardening I sowed Jersey Wakefield in late August/early September as Bob Gill advised, and harvested them in April as green and golden glories. They didn't all head up but they sure were tasty.

Last year at Pragtree Farm they froze out at 15°F. This year we sowed them in a cold frame. We will overwinter them there and plant them out in February. I read about this technique in Neuhof's *Cole Crops* (see page 125) and it seems worth trying.

You can also sow Jersey Wakefield and Golden Acre in flats or a cold frame in March and plant out in April (although that is the worst time for root fly maggot). These head up in midsummer, of course, which is beyond the scope of this book.

A word of caution to city gardeners: from what I've observed in Seattle, it's a lot harder to get good cabbages in the city. Either they are too crowded, or they are more sensitive to pollution and lower light levels, or something. Be sure to give them rich soil, lime it well, give them plenty of moisture while they are young, and plenty of room (18 inches apart either way in beds, or 36 inches between the rows if you have the space to do row gardening).

Cauliflower

B. oleracea botrytis Half Hardy

Purple Giant (DAM)
St. Valentine (TIL) - white, but really a "broccoli"
Veitch Autumn Giant (ABL, A&B,TIL)
Veitch Self Protecting (A&B-as broccoli, T&M)

Cauliflowers are known as hard to grow, but I feel a lot of that comes from trying to grow them for the summer. If the aim is to produce them for the fall, winter, and spring, and the right varieties are used, they become less of a problem.

However, there *are* still difficulties, especially if you leave them too long in the nursery bed, don't feed and water them enough or, with the overwintering ones, don't give them enough time to put on size before the winter. These stresses will cause them to button up (make stunted heads) or, with varieties that are closest to their sprouting broccoli ancestors, send up leaves in the head.

If you are a beginning gardener, you might want to avoid cauliflowers in the first year and devote your space to a more productive and reliable crop. They are low in Vitamin A in comparison with other crucifers (though fair in other nutrients) and the winter varieties take up lots of space—3 ft. either way.

If you decide to grow them, make sure your soil is well composted, that you water them well in dry spells and, if you use a nursery bed, transplant them before they get crowded. Both Simons and Hills have good sections on cauliflowers. See chart on previous page.

Purple Giant

We are trying out Purple Giant from Dam this year. At this early November writing it is large, with many lateral shoots which will, I suppose, turn into small heads if the plants don't freeze out. It was sown in June with the rest of the main and late crop brassicas; the dry spell we had then didn't seem to set it back at all. Other purple and green cauliflowers that I've tried have not done well for me, but I think I put them in too early.

St. Valentine (TIL)

The traditional cauliflower for March to May is St. Valentine. I've discussed it under broccoli where Tillinghast lists it. You can't tell a

St. Valentine from a Snowball by the way it looks, only by the way it behaves. It's much slower growing, hardier (though not much), and tends to sprout after the main head is cut.

Veitch Autumn Giant

Veitch Autumn Giants, sown in my Seattle garden in June, gave huge heads from October to January. I also sowed some in August, and got heads from March to May, but they were smaller—of a regular Snowball size.

Chinese Cabbage

B. pekinensis var cylindrica Half Hardy

Chefoo (ABL)
China King (JSS)
Michihli (ABL)
Wintertime (STK)

China King
Wintertime

Big commercial grade heads from an early August sowing. Last through to a hard frost (approximately 18°F). They seem resistant to root fly maggot—they may get infested but keep on producing. China King and Wintertime are hybrids and transplant well, unlike other Chinese cabbages.

Chefoo
Michihli

These two make smaller heads and seem more set back by the cabbage root fly maggot. They are also harder to grow than the oriental greens, so I don't bother with them any more. I had to admit to a prejudiced palate—I prefer the European brassicas! But I have noticed that the Asian ones do seem to be better stir-fry material.

Collards

B. oleracea var acephala Very Hardy
Vates (ABL,STK)

These small open cabbages, popular in the South and in Black communities, are very useful as greens in the late winter. I have read that they were known as coleworts in England, and used especially in late winter. I suspect, though, that both collards and coleworts were names for many different forms of small, loose, and open growing cabbages. I don't know which varieties have come down to us.

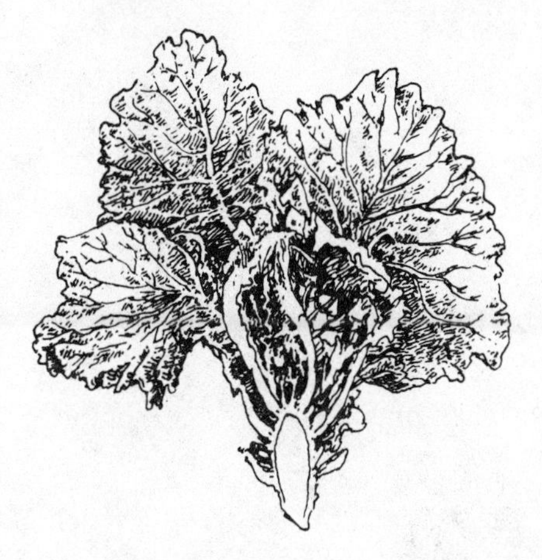

Collards are being tested this year at Pragtree Farm for cold hardiness. They go through most Seattle winters well. They can be sown up till July 15th for a good crop. Abundant Life Seeds has a local variety of Vates for sale, and there might be other good hardy varieties in the south that would do well here. It would be good to see if some can be located by the True Seed Exchange (see page 123).

I have heard of a variety in Seattle called Tree Collards, but seed isn't available commercially. The ones we have look very much like a primitive cabbage, and in the 30-odd plants that are growing I can see hints of kohlrabi, Marrowstem kale, red cabbage, etc.

Cress

Barbarea verna/praecox (?) Very Hardy
American Winter Cress (SGC,ABL)

Lepidium sativum Half Hardy
Cress (SGC,ABL)
Peppergrass (SGC, ABL)

You often find *Barbarea verna* (American Winter Cress)

growing wild. In fact, it has thoroughly naturalized itself in my old Seattle garden where I started it from seed one fall, and then ignored it because I found I didn't like it much. It tastes rather like a hot watercress. A small innocuous plant, it would do well in the herb garden where you could just let it be and gather small amounts for winter salads.

Lepidium sativum, the other cress, is more succulent, and is often grown for sprouts (as well as outside) in Europe. Hills has a good description of how to do this under a cardboard box!

Kale

B. *oleracea* — Very Hardy

- Dwarf Scotch Curled (ABL,DAM,TIL)
- Green Curled Scotch (A&B)
- Semi-Dwarf Green Curled (DAM,TIL)
- Tall Green Curled (DAM)
- Tall Scotch Curled (ABL)
- Thousand Headed (ABL,A&B)

B. *campestris**

- Dwarf Siberian (ABL,TIL,JSS)

Good for Livestock

- Marrowstem (DAM)
- Thousand Headed (ABL,A&B)

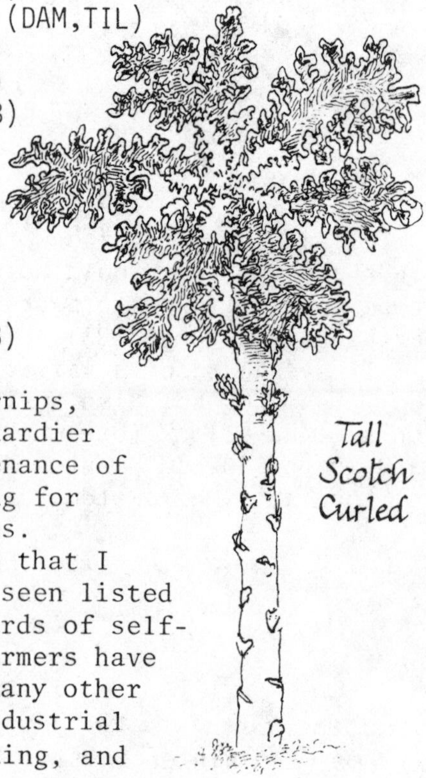

Tall Scotch Curled

Kale, along with leeks, turnips, Brussels sprouts, and the hardier cabbages, formed the maintenance of late winter vegetable eating for Europeans for many centuries.

There are many varieties that I have read about (but never seen listed in catalogues). Old standards of self-sufficient gardeners and farmers have disappeared along with so many other good varieties since the Industrial Revolution, freezers, trucking, and

* I can't find this listed and suspect it must be an alternate name for B. *rapa* or B. *napus*, as Hills says it is the ancestor of turnip and rutabaga. Brassica taxonomy sure must be a can o' worms!

a change in eating patterns. But kale, thougn you might not find it in the supermarkets, is high in Vitamins A, E, and K and being so hardy, merits attention, if not midwinter devotion, and a place in your garden.

Hills says there are two forms of kale. The first stems from B. *oleracea*, and includes Dwarf and Tall Scotch, Semi-Dwarf and Tall Curled, and Thousand Headed. Thousand Headed is huge and used for stock. The others (which seem to me to be just one variety in tall and dwarf) are good for small gardens as they can be started in flats and put out at their normal spacing (24 inches between plants) when needed.

The second form of kale does not transplant well. It stems from B. *campestris* and includes Siberian, Russian, Hengry Gap, and Asparagus kale. I haven't found the last two in retail catalogues, but I got some Russian seed from Wendy Bender, and Abundant Life may be able to list it soon.

B. campestris can be sown directly in July or August, and needs plenty of room—24 inches between plants, and 30 inches between rows. If you are worried about germination, you can sow a few extra seeds and then thin, feeding the discards to the stock in September. Don't manure or compost before you sow; the plants will grow too fast and not be as hardy, which is what you want them for.

Siberian Kale

If you are a small family or have a small garden, you probably only need a few plants as you crop these on the "cut and come again" principle. Take only a few bottom leaves or sprouts at a time from each plant.

I like Dwarf Siberian best for eating raw, especially in the early spring when the new sprouts and leaves are very tender. Some folk I know eat Scotch and the Green Curled varieties raw too, but I find them tough and strong flavored, even though they do improve after a frost. I prefer them in soups and stews where they are delicious. Russian is a reddish-purple colored one, and tastes mild like Siberian even in the fall.

Kohlrabi

B. oleracea caulorapa Half Hardy
Purple Vienna (ABL,SGC)
White Vienna (ABL,SGC)

Kohlrabi isn't that hardy, but if you like it I suppose it's worth having till it freezes out. If it doesn't and you leave it be, it will send up nice shoots in the spring that taste and look like raab.

Kohlrabi is fairly high in Vitamin A (higher than cabbage, lower than kale; Hills, p. 133), but low in C. I think it's fairly good in salads and stir-fries. You can direct sow it in the middle of July. The Purple ones seem much slower growing.

Mustards

B. chinensis var chinensis Half Hardy
Chinese Pak-Choi/Bok Choy (ABL,JSS,T&MI)

B. juncea var crispifolium
Green Wave (JSS)

B. juncea var rugosa, foliosa, etc.
India Mustards (SGC,T&M)

B. pekinensis
Tai Tsai

Mizuna (ABL,JSS)

Tendergreen (ABL)

I haven't found any good thorough discussion of the origin and taxonomy of mustards yet, so I'm just listing the above as they come in seed catalogues and hope for clarification later.

I've tested Pak-Choi, Mizuna, and Tai Tsai and they go to roughly 18°F. They are the milder ones, good for salads as well as steaming and stir-fries.

For a late crop of Pak-Choi, Mizuna, and Tai Tsai, I sow in mid to late August and let them go to frost, not bothering much with them because there is so much else at that time of year.

Unfortunately, there is a heavy root fly laying most Augusts. If it's rainy or you keep them wet, they will make it through. A cold frame or greenhouse sowing in late February/early March will give

you a good early crop of greens before the fly hits. I haven't tried India Mustard, Tendergreen, or Green Wave. The sowing dates are the same as the varieties above. Tendergreen is apparently good for spring. The plants taste hotter than Pak-Choi, Mizuna, and Tai Tsai and they have broader, hairy leaves.

Raab

Brassica (?) Half Hardy
Raab/Rapa (SGC)

Raab is a nice little overwintering sprouting "broccoli" from Italy. The ones I've grown don't look like broccoli at all in the leaf stage. Raab does not have the powdery greyish blue or green cast that gives a glaucous quality to broccoli. Instead, it is hairy with a mustard-like appearance. I haven't found any taxonomic references on it yet. Sow it from late August to mid-September for an early spring crop. Good in stir-fries.

Radish

Raphanus sativum Hardy
any varieties and sources

China Rose, Daikon, and the other oriental radishes can be sown in mid-July, the Black Spanish in early August. I found both types rather hot and full of maggots, so I stick with the regular early spring types which I sow in late August and mid-September. They go past Thanksgiving, sometimes to Christmas. Slugs love them.

Rocket

Eruca sativa Hardy (?)

Rocket (DAM, SGC, Five Corners)

Rocket is another of the small wild-like brassicas of which I personally am not fond. You can find a good description of it in Pellegrini's book, *The Food Lover's Garden* (Read, page 124).

Below is a response from a friend who read my comments about Rocket in the manuscript. It is a perfect example of the individuality of tastes and gardens.

> *"(Rocket was) my first crop and absolutely delicious despite your disdain! Try it in pocket bread with hummus or in salad with feta cheese and you'll become a convert. The slugs didn't touch it, which I suppose is why it was my first crop. (It has beautiful flowers too!)"* Judy Munger

Rutabaga

B. *napus var napobrassica* Hardy (?)

Laurention

I don't grow this because I prefer the nonbrassica roots, so I can only refer you to Bob Gill who says to plant them from July 1-15. It seems to me that in many locations, the earlier date would be better to avoid the root fly maggot, especially if you mulch the young plants well. I have little experience with them left in the ground, but rutabagas do store well.

Turnip

B. *rapa* Very Hardy (?)

Purple Top White Globe (ABL,STK)

Turnips kept in the ground quite nicely for us during the winter of '76-'77, tasting as good as turnips ever do through 9° frost. They didn't get woody until around February/March. They were sown in early August (a sowing later than August 15 will produce mostly tops).

In Seattle's Black community, turnips are planted very early in the year (February), mostly for greens. Plenty of ashes are put along the rows, and the first harvests are made from thinnings in late March. The whole plants are taken in April, when the roots are the size of marbles, till they are as big as gold balls.

I don't much care for turnips, so if *you do* you probably know far more than I. Why not write in and let us know, and we'll put the information in the next edition of the book. While you're at it, tell us about rutabagas too! If you want to read about them, Hills, Simons, and Thompson & Kelly all have interesting general things to say.

Watercress

Nasturtium officionale Very Hardy
Watercress (ABL,SGC)

This is a perennial found in ditches and streams of even such cold areas as the Midwest. Watercress should be easy to start from either seed or cuttings, though I haven't tried it. You might be able to get a bunch of it from a farmer at the Pike Street Market in Seattle and try rooting it in very moist sand. It will produce well in any place with rich soil that you can keep moist through the summer.

ALLIUMS

Onions

Allium cepa Hardy
Bulb onion for sets (SGC, et al.)

A. cepa aggregatum
Multiplier/Potato onion
Shallots

A. cepa proliferum Very Hardy
Multiplier Top Sets (ABL)/Top Onion/Tree Onion

The alliums include various types of onions, as well as leeks, shallots, and scallions.

Writing about onions proved to be very difficult. There is much confusion in the literature over nomenclature. For example, I found three different appearing types of onions all having the same name. Also, different growers and seeds people, all of equal competence, had different and fixed opinions about which variety was best for when. It seems that onions are at a point of rapid evolutionary development, difficult even for the taxonomist, let alone the gardener, to keep up with.

I don't hope to shed any more light on the subject. I only hope that I don't confuse it more. For taxonomy, I consulted the most modern book I could find, *The Oxford Book of Food Plants*. It is English, and there may be some usages that differ from this country. I hope to find out more for the next edition.

ONIONS FOR GREENS

There are several ways to have onion greens all winter. One is to plant sets of any variety of the regular bulbing onion (*A. cepa*) available from most gardening stores (including Seattle Garden Center), from late August through October. Then cut the tops or pull them as you wish through the winter. Any leftovers will bolt in the spring. This is the easy, but expensive way. They are "Hardy".

Another way is to get some Top (or Egyptian, or Tree) onions. A. *cepa viviparum* is their old Latin name, but the Oxford book now places them in a group called *proliferum*. These propagate in two ways:

1) By topsets, or bulblets (little bulbs that form at the top of the stalk where the flower should be, or sometimes in coexistence with them). These you can harvest in midsummer when they are ripe and plant for greens in the fall. They will then turn into next year's mature onions. The stalks will die down, leaving the big bulbs in the soil.

2) Harvest three or four of the big bulbs, leaving one in place to multiply. Or harvest them all and select out the best to replant for reproduction. These bulbs are strong flavored, and at their best when dug from the soil in midwinter.

Once you have these growing in your garden, you should have them for a long time as they are very persistent, "very hardy", and don't require much attention, even weeding. I had top onions in my Wisconsin garden, and they propagated themselves happily there, year after year, going through minus thirty degree freezes and three feet of snow. You might find these from gardening neighbors, and ABL carries them as Multiplier Top Sets.

There are two other types of onions that will send up greens all winter if you plant them in the fall, though they are more usually grown for their small bulbs. The first is the Potato Onion, also known as Multiplier, and sometimes sold as Shallots because they are in the same group, A. *aggregatum* (previously they were listed as A. *cepa solanium*). They are yellow in color and their bulbs tend to be big, round, and taste like the regular onions of commerce. I don't know where you can find seed or bulbs for propagation.

The second type you can use for greens are shallots themselves, previously classed as their own species (A. *ascalonicum*) but now grouped by *Oxford Book of Food Plants* as A. *cepa aggregatum*. Whatever they are called, they sure taste good, meatier and less sharp or oniony. Some "shallots" you find for sale are yellow skinned, but the ones that are said around here to originate in France have a pinkish brownish hue, and I think taste the best.

After they are through making greens they die down, and you can then use the bulbs in the late spring when you are out of regular bulb onions.

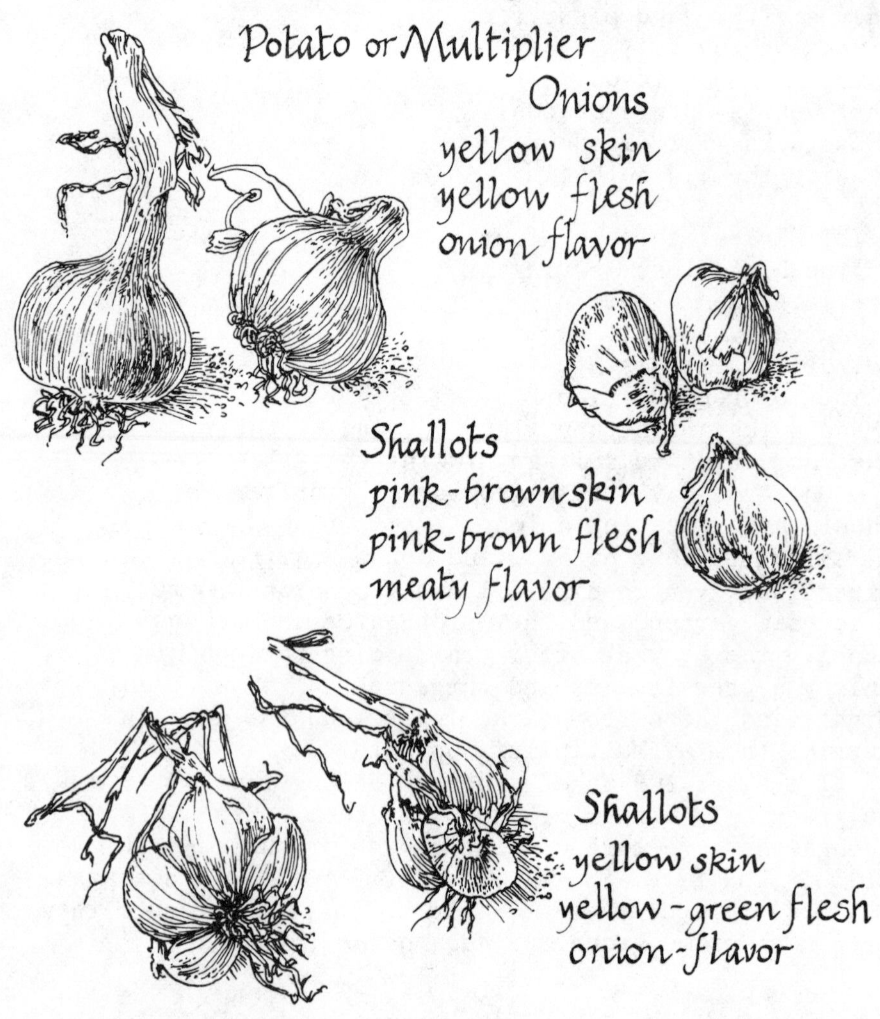

EARLY BULBS

A. *cepa* Hardy-Very Hardy

Kaizuka (JSS)
Senshyu Yellow (A&B, hybrid)

We tried the Kaizukas last year, and they did okay with lousy soil and no attention to speak of, producing nice bulbs by May from an August sowing. If you are going to try these I suggest you make the traditional efforts for a good onion bed (complete directions are in Simons or Hills) and sow half in late July, half in early to mid-August to see which produce best for you.

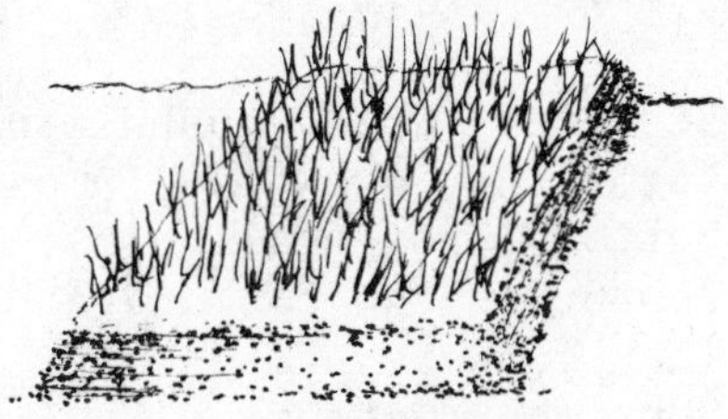

traditional onion bed

Leeks

Very Hardy

A. *ampeloprasum var. porrum*

Carentian
Giant Mussleburg (STK)
Unique (JSS)
Winterleek (ABL)

Leeks are a standard winter crop in Europe and the British Isles, but not so well known to most Americans. Sow early in the spring in flats, or by April in beds or rows. Thin to two inches on-center. They mature by fall and stand till April before bolting. If you let a few go to seed, they will be beautiful and will save you seed money. The seed is easy to collect, but won't keep beyond a year. The stalk from which you take the seed will have a couple of little bulbs at the bottom, and these can be used for propagation.

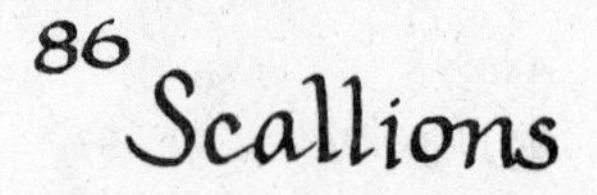

Scallions

A. *fistulosum* — Very Hardy (?)

Evergreen Nabuka (ABL)
Evergreen Sakata (JSS)
Hardy White Bunching (STK)
Prosperity (JSS)

Scallions are a nonbulbing perennial. In their original form, they grow in clumps with small, slightly swollen bottoms, not real bulbs. In this form they were for centuries the common garden onion of China and Japan. They flower in midsummer and then die down. With the September/October rains, they start growing and are usable again. There are now many horticultural varieties which are grown for market as annuals. These are supposed to overwinter well and I'm trying them this winter.

Beans

Phaseolus coccineus — Half Hardy (root only)

Scarlet Runner

P. *vulgaris* — Not Hardy

Bush Beans
- Purple Pod
- Tendergreen (ABL)

P. *vulgaris* — Not Hardy

Pole Beans
- Bluelake
- Kentucky Wonder
- Oregon Giant (ABL)
- Romano

In Seattle my late pole beans (trained up a south wall) cropped till Thanksgiving. I planted them in the first week of July. Bob Gill says you can plant bush beans till July 25th but I never tried them as I prefer the poles for flavor and tenderness. Out in the foothills, the first October frost took the July plantings as well as the June ones which were still producing, so it doesn't seem worth the effort if you live in similar cold areas. Myrna Twomey on Whidbey reports that July sowings of beans do not produce for her (though peas do).

The roots of Scarlet Runner will sometimes overwinter in Seattle and the shore areas and it, like Purple Pod Bush, does better in cooler soils than the others. The pods tend to be fibrous, though, and should be eaten when small. If, however, you don't get the pods picked in time, the seeds (which are streaked with purple and pink) are excellent.

Vicia faba Hardy

Fava Beans

Long Pod (A&B)
Windsor (T&M,JSS)
Windsor Long Pod (STK)

Fava beans are wonderful, tasty, early legumes, which are quite different from the common garden bean *Phaseolus*. Long used in the Mediterranean, Northern Europe, and Asia, they are the perfect cool season legume.

Hills says that there are two basic varieties of fava beans: the Long Pod type, for sowing in November (Solly and Bob Gill say November 10th), and the Windsor type for February (or March if you don't have black aphid or black fly in your area). Simons says he thinks the November sowing is useless if you live in a hard frost area, and I tend to agree because the November sowing I did at Pragtree was mostly lost, to either frost or mice, presumably the former.

However, Pragtree has no black fly, so the February/March sowings did well. This aphid overwinters on Bigleaf maples, so if you have those in your district and they are infested, you're probably better off with the November sowing.

In Seattle, where the fly is prevalent, I did a January sowing that produced fairly well. In this sort of situation you can cut back the tender tops which the aphids infest.

In either case, favas are ready before the *Phaseolus* beans (and sometimes before the peas). I find them best when the seeds are the size of a large thumbnail as later the skin gets tough (though the seed inside still tastes good). Some folk eat the pods when they are the size of small *Phaseolus* beans, but I find them bitter.

Beets

Beta vulgaris Hardy

Lutz (ABL)
Winterkeeper (STK)

Winterkeeper and Lutz are two favorites, but almost any of the small beet varieties will do also (e.g., Detroit). Winterkeepers should be planted in late June/early July so that they will have time to mature their tender, sweet, *big* roots. Their leaves are pale green and sweet, too. Lutz is a green leaf beet also, but it doesn't have any root to speak of. Both of these varieties should be mulched if you have frosts that go much below 15°F, so plant in rows.

Burdock

Arctium minus Very Hardy

Takinogawa (ABL,JSS)
Watanabe (JSS)

I used to collect burdock wild in the Midwest. It is strange tasting but good. The Italians and the Asians place great store in its medicinal qualities.

Sow in the spring (it's a slow grower) and gather from fall onwards. However, don't let it go to seed and escape to your land; it's a pernicious weed and if you have sheep the burrs will make the wool unusable.

Cardoons

Cynara cardunculus (DAM, SGC)

Half Hardy

Cardoons are a tall relative of globe artichokes. In the fall, their stalks must be blanched even higher than celery by wrapping with paper. When blanched in this way, they will stand until December. Simons, *The Oxford Book of Food Plants*, and especially Pellegrini have good descriptions of how to grow these. If you like the taste of globe artichokes, you will also like cardoons.

Cardoons are sown in May and harvested in November. After the first harvest in the fall, you can let them overwinter for a good final crop in spring. The seeds generally don't mature this far north.

You can see some cardoon plants in the Drug & Herb Garden at the University of Washington, but they have not been blanched for eating.

Carrots

Dauca carota

Hardy

Frubund (T&M)

In my first garden in Seattle, I inadvertently left carrots in the ground all winter and they were great till April. Unfortunately, every other place I've gardened in the Northwest has been infested with Carrot Rust Fly Maggot (see page 46), a nasty relative of the Cabbage Root Fly maggot. When these attack, they leave long grey and rust colored tunnels that make the carrot bitter.

Elsewhere the carrots had wireworm damage, which is almost as bad, so I harvest them and store in damp sand or peat. If you don't have the fly or wireworm and want to store carrots in the ground, mulch them well for they are ruined by freezing lower than 15°.

Frubund is carried this year by T&M and described as the "first genuine Autumn sowing carrot" for an early spring crop. They often carry novelties like this for only one year, so I'm dubious but am still going to try it. Forest Glenn Roth of Abudant Life Seeds points out that spring cropping is possible with many carrot varieties; you just have to get the planting date right—late August/early September. I haven't tried it.

Celeriac

Apium graveolens var rapaceum Hardy

Giant Prague (ABL,JSS)

I have to admit that I've had small success with celeriac (or "root celery"), although it's one of my favorites. I suspect that my problem was in not having rich enough starting soil (see celery below), irregular watering while in flats, crowding, and not enough water in the final bed. Myrna Twomey harvests the roots till March from her garden but many sources say to lift and store celeriac in peat in the fall.

Celery

Apium graveolens Half Hardy

Florimart (STK)
Heung Kunn (TM&I)
Leaf Celery (DAM)
Smallage (ABL)
Utah 52-70 (ABL,STK)

In my Seattle garden, most Utah celery plants overwintered without any difficulty; just a few frozen outer leaves. They tasted very strong and bitter though, being mostly good for soups and stews, but *very* good for that! A few plants lived three years, which surprised me since they are supposed to be biennial. I suppose it's because I took the center flower stalk to eat before it bloomed.

CELERY MULCH

Much below 18°F the centers die out, so if you live in a cold spot and want to carry them over, try a high mulch (or putting them in cold frames, cloches, or plastic sheds). If the outer leaves die back before you use them, be sure to take them off. Mushy rotten stalks will eventually rot the core of the plant.

I'm trying the other three celery varieties for the first time this winter. I suspect they must be all fairly similar—at least they taste that way. They are smaller in the stalk than regular celery, closer to the ground, and have a stronger flavor. They may also prove a bit hardier.

Sow all varieties between February and April in a cold frame or in greenhouse flats, keeping them very moist in very rich soil. (Try 2 inches of potting soil on top of well rotted manure.) Plant out in May/June. If you missed and have to start late or get plants from another grower, don't worry, you can get a good fall crop even from July transplants.

Chickweed

Stellaria media — Very Hardy
Chickweed (ABL)

A "weed" of most garden soils, chickweed makes an excellent living green mulch for Brussels sprouts and broccolis, though it rather overwhelms lettuce and onions if you have good soil.

In fact, the size of the leaf indicates the fertility of the soil—as big as watercress, fantastic! A side effect of growing chickweed on rich soils is that the bigger leaves are more succulent and have a better flavor. I clip the stems with scissors to avoid pulling the lower parts of the runners out of the dirt.

If by some chance you don't have chickweed in your garden, you should be able to get runners from a neighbor in the late fall when the rains start, which is when it puts on its best growth.

Dear Binda,

Did you know that chickweed (stellaria media) was still a real vegetable in medieval times? I once read an old guild statute, where all the different courses of a meal were described, which the wife of a Master Craftsman had to serve to the journeymen and there was also Mierlein or chickweed mentioned. How times change!

Ute Grimlund,
Marysville, Washington

Chicory

Chicorium intybus Hardy

Root
- Whitloof Improved (French endive) (STK)

Leaf
- Snowflake (T&M)
- Sugarhat (Burpee)
- Sugarloaf (B&M)

Root chicory grows like a regular lettuce (but it's *very slow*). It is then lifted in the fall (when you have time) and stored in the root cellar in a box of dry sand. When you want some sprouts, just take a few roots, put them in a box of wet sand and cut off the funny, slightly bitter cones as they get to size (about 5-inches). These used to sell back East for extravagant prices. I've never found the energy to do this later part of the game, though I've grown the tops three years running. They did well through the winter in Seattle, but froze out at about 12°F last year at Pragtree Farm. The leaf chicories I have not grown, though reports are they are hardy.

Corn Salad

Valerianella olitoria Very Hardy
Corn Salad (ABL,SGC,T&M)

Corn salad was derived from a weed in the "corn" (grain) fields of Europe. It is very succulent and improves with the season, something a lettuce doesn't do.

In April it sends up little flowering stalks which are just as edible as in the fall; delicious and never bitter. The plants are small, low to the ground, and take some time to pick and wash but I think it's worth it. It used to be a commercial crop in Europe; maybe it still is.

If you want it for the fall, broadcast seed in late July. Otherwise, broadcast by August 15th for the cooler districts and the first part of September for the cities. Two sq.ft. should handle a small family unless you become addicted to it. For the first half of the winter, you can just cut the large outer leaves; then start taking whole plants as they shoot up.

If you want to save your own seeds, spread a newspaper under the plants to catch them as the plant ripens a little at a time over a month. Clean the paper off every few days, and store the seed. M. Vilmorin-Andrieux (in *The Vegetable Garden*, 1860) says that the seed, like that of squashes and cucumbers, is better the second year.

corn salad

Endive - Escarole

Chichorium endiva Hardy

Endive (ABL,JSS,STK)

I haven't grown either endive or escarole. I'm not fond of curly endive, but I *do* like the loose open heads of escarole I buy from Italian farmers in the Pike Place Market. Elaine Davenport, who has grown it in the Leschi district of Seattle, says it is almost as hardy as cabbage (probably down to 18°) and loses its bitterness as it keeps on growing through the winter. Sow till the middle of July.

Florence Fennel

Foeniculum vulgare var dulce Half Hardy (?)

Florence Fennel (ABL)

This plant is a real sleeper. Italian in origin and not often found for sale, Florence Fennel is worthy of more attention by local gardeners and cooks. Sown in early to mid-July, it makes a funny swollen base to the leaf stalks rather like celery. You break the stalks, cut off the leaves, and steam or saute in a little butter. Marvelous and succulent. The root is good too.

I avoided Florence Fennel at first, because I'm not terribly fond of fennel seed flavor, but this almost disappears in the cooking. I'm testing its hardiness this winter. It will probably go to at least 18°F.

Good King Henry

Chenopodium bonus henricus Very Hardy
Good King Henry (H&H)

I haven't grown or tasted this, but I'm very fond of its relative C. *album* (Fat Hen, Lambs Quarters, Goosefoot) which is an annual weed of the summer garden. Good King Henry is a perennial which shoots up early in the spring. You eat the stalks like asparagus or, if you wait till later, eat the leaves like spinach. It will do well in any rich garden soil (in the perennial section, of course).

I read about it in Simons and Sherwell-Cooper, but it's taken me a long time to find seeds. They are available from the University Botanic Garden, Oxford, England. If you like Lambs Quarters and want to try this one, ask for a sample of seed (it's free) under its Latin name. Good luck!

Jerusalem Artichoke

Helianthus tuberosum Very Hardy

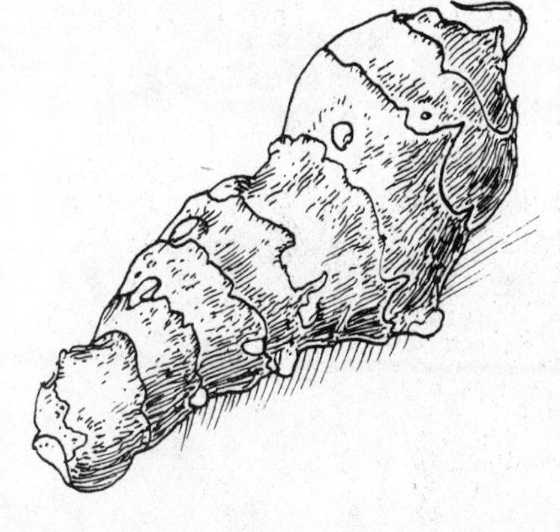

This perennial species of sunflower produces a large quantity of tubers that should be left in the ground all winter. They are very "weedy" and tall and belong well away from or to the north of the rest of the garden. They are good raw in salads, or lightly sauteed, but not boiled as they are even easier than potatoes to overcook.

Get some healthy looking tubers from a local coop or supplier whenever they are available. They can be planted in the ground anytime you get them, from October till February, but they won't be ready for eating till the following fall. Then they can be dug from October till April, but don't lift more than you can use in a day, as they turn soft very rapidly. Slugs like them, but the plants almost always produce more tubers than you can possible eat.

Lettuce

Latuca sativa Half Hardy

Almost every type of lettuce I've tried in Seattle did well outside through the winters, and at Pragtree in cold frames. Varieties included oakleaf, bibb varieties, buttercrunch, Grand Rapids, Fulton, cos (romaine), Prizehead, Celtuce, and Ruby. They all lived through frosts of 18°F and were productive, although slow, from mid-August sowings. They got bitter after December, but I found I didn't mind; I dislike paying money for California Wilted Wonders.

LD Hills recommends Winter Density (JSS), a romaine, for before Christmas, but at Pragtree it froze out around 17°F. For after Christmas, he says Arctic King (T&M) is the hardiest. This is a slow growing butterhead type tinged with brown, like prizehead. It is being tried by a few of the Winter Garden Project gardeners around the Sound this year.

If you live out of the city, I think that it pays to have a plastic shed, cloche, or cold frame for lettuce. You get better and more productive plants that way. There's a big difference between a miserable lettuce that's just hanging in there, and one that's producing lots of leaves, or whole heads, for you to eat. Of course, if you have a greenhouse, I suppose you're already growing lettuce! (See *Solar Greenhouse*, page 127)

August 15th sowings grow to a good size for fall and winter; September ones can be sown for late winter and spring in a protection device. These later ones can be moved into a greenhouse or hot frame for rapid growth in February/March.

Parsley

Petroselinum crispum Very Hardy

Curled (any seed co.)
Plain (Italian) (any seed co.)

Although plain and curled varieties are hardy, I think the plain (which is the original form) maintains color better, produces more, and suffers less damage from cold and rain. Both are biennial, so you have to start new plants every year. They set seed easily and germination is better with the home grown plants in my experience. If you are growing both varieties, only let one set seed because they cross.

You don't have to keep the seed in a package over winter; just broadcast it into a bed when it is ready, and thin after germination in the fall.

Parsnip

Pastinaca sativa Very Hardy
any variety

Plant parsnips in May for big roots, or up till June for carrot-sized ones. Just leave them in the ground and pull as needed after the first frost. They will bolt in March/April. Carrot rust fly doesn't seem to attack them too badly, nor ruin the taste.

Peas

Pisum sativum Not Hardy
any 60 day variety of English Vine or Snow Pea

A fall crop from a mid-July sowing isn't as big as a spring one, but the peas should produce till frost. Keep well watered. Some people do an October/November sowing for very early and healthy spring crops (April/May). T&M have a fall-sown variety—Winfrieda—which they say is good. Abundant Life and the Seattle Garden Center will usually have peas for summer and fall sowing.

Potatoes

Solanum tuberosum
any variety
Hardy

In Seattle I always left my few potatoes in the ground because I didn't have any better storage place, and because they always tasted fresh—like 'new' potatoes. Slugs are a hazard, however. They can destroy half a crop while you're toasting your toes before the fire by burrowing down in the soil or mulch to get the tubers. So if you are dependent on your potatoes for staple, I think it's wiser to store them in the regular manner. Burying potatoes in damp sand or peat will keep them almost as fresh as leaving them in the ground. Keep your "seed" potatoes separate.

Salsify

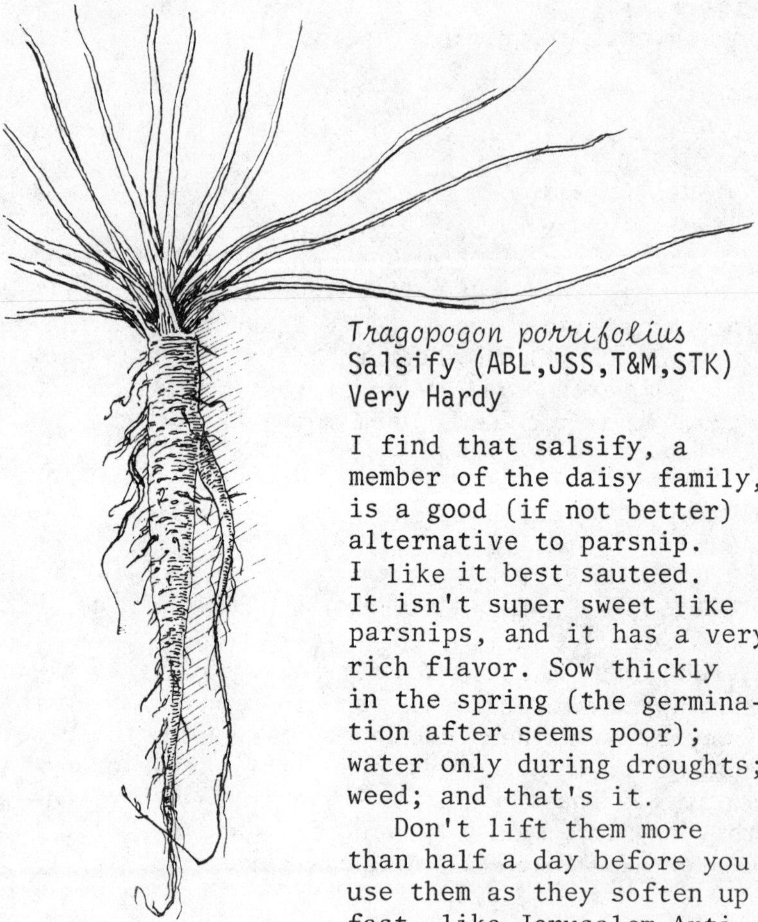

Tragopogon porrifolius
Salsify (ABL,JSS,T&M,STK)
Very Hardy

I find that salsify, a member of the daisy family, is a good (if not better) alternative to parsnip. I like it best sauteed. It isn't super sweet like parsnips, and it has a very rich flavor. Sow thickly in the spring (the germination after seems poor); water only during droughts; weed; and that's it.

Don't lift them more than half a day before you use them as they soften up fast, like Jerusalem Artichokes . In the spring the new leaves are good as a cooked or salad green. Salsify is biennial, so if you want to save your own seed, just leave one plant and it will shoot up to 4-5 ft. in May and show its purple flowers through June mornings. The seeds come in a ball like dandelions, so catch them before they shatter in a wind, on dry July days.

Scorzonera

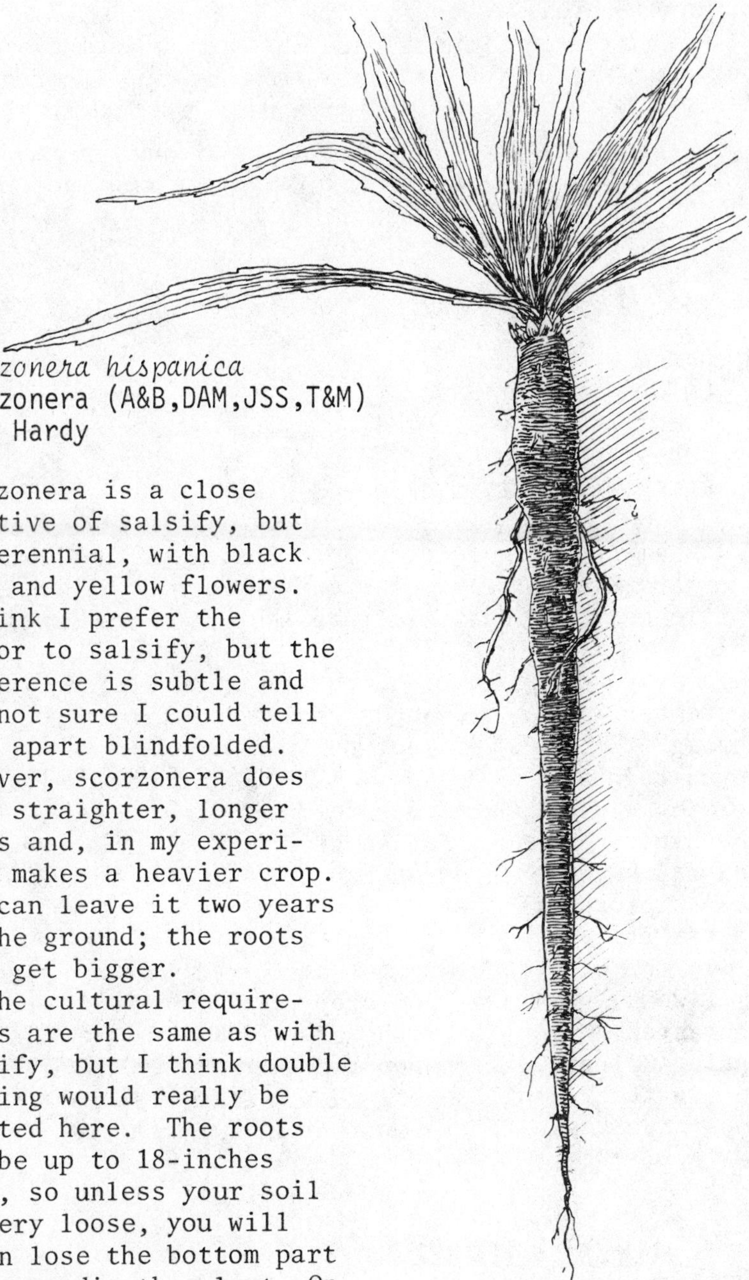

Scorzonera hispanica
Scorzonera (A&B,DAM,JSS,T&M)
Very Hardy

Scorzonera is a close relative of salsify, but is perennial, with black skin and yellow flowers. I think I prefer the flavor to salsify, but the difference is subtle and I'm not sure I could tell them apart blindfolded. However, scorzonera does have straighter, longer roots and, in my experience makes a heavier crop. You can leave it two years in the ground; the roots just get bigger.

The cultural requirements are the same as with salsify, but I think double digging would really be merited here. The roots can be up to 18-inches long, so unless your soil is very loose, you will often lose the bottom part when you dig the plant. On the other hand, if you don't have the time, strength, or weather to double dig a bed in April, don't worry.

The roots will get down into the subsoil by themselves, drawing up valuable nutrients for you to eat in January and February.

Cultural requirements are the same as salsify with one caution: if you have plantain growing in your garden, it will be hard to distinguish the two in the seedling stage. The differences are that scorzonera has serrated edges to its leaves and a downiness on the inner surfaces.

Spinach

Spinacea oleracea Very Hardy

- Cold Resistant Savoy (STK)
- Giant Winter (ABL,DAM)
- Longstanding Winter (T&M)
- Prickly (Giant Thickleaved) (A&B)

I was amazed at how hardy Cold Resistant Savoy was in our garden last year. It went through 9° frost with little damage. Beats lettuce (but has more oxalic acid).

A July sowing in rich, moist soil will feed you in September, and a mid-August sowing will last you through till you get your new plants up in the spring. Seven to nine inches apart is a good distance for spacing winter plants. Water well if it is dry while the plants are small; then stop to let them harden off. Don't plant more than you can eat, and keep the outer leaves picked if they die or yellow before you want to eat them.

In the city to close to water, a September planting will work. I had a good crop of Giant Winter in Leschi. It lasted so long it might as well be called "Giant Spring Spinach". I haven't tested its cold-hardiness out in the foothills yet, though Cold Resistant Savoy does have a sweeter taste than Giant Winter in the fall.

Swiss Chard

Beta vulgaris var cicla Very Hardy

- Lucullus (ABL,etc.)

This is one of the few vegetables that you can regularly see overwintering in gardens around the Northwest.

In English catalogues it is called Perpetual Spinach or Spinach Beet. The '76 crop at Pragtree lived through the coldest weather, and it was sown in June. But if you don't eat it during the summer, a July sowing will suffice.

Keep the chard well trimmed, taking off the outer leaves right down to the soil even if you don't eat them. If they freeze and turn mushy, they might rot the rest of the plant.

Herbs

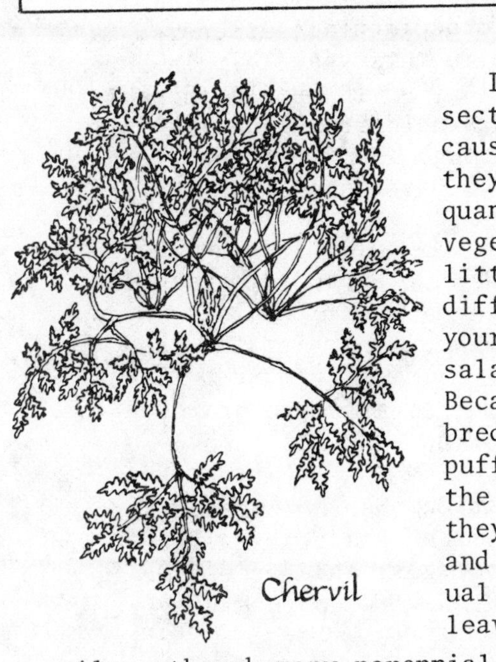

Chervil

I'm putting herbs in a section of their own because, being more powerful, they aren't used in the quantities of the other vegetables, and it's that little bit that makes the difference, especially to your winter and spring salads, sauces, and soups. Because they haven't been bred to be all soft and puffed up the way we like the rest of our vegetables, they have more vitamins and minerals (and spiritual essence?) in their leaves.

Also, though many perennial herbs die somewhat in the depth of our winters, they stay late and come back early. Their earliness is especially welcome for meals served in the doldrums of March and April. You can disguise cabbage with a lemon thyme sauce, or revolutionize the same old salad with new lovage sprouts. Most of the herbs mentioned below are known for their medicinal properties as well as their culinary virtues, so that's another good reason to have them available for winter consumption.

Chervil

Anthriscus cerefolium Very Hardy
Chervil (ABL,JSS,MB,SGC)

I really like this small licorice tasting plant. Chervil gives a surprising taste to winter salads and it's no bother as it self-sows in late summer. To start it off, sow the seeds in good soil in late July/August, and water till the plants are established.

Chinese Leek - Garlic Chives

A. *tuberosum* Hardy
Chinese Leek/Garlic Chives (ABL,JSS,TM&I)

This is relatively new to occidental gardeners, and I tried it for the first time this year. It is perennial and seems *very* slow growing, so it should probably be started early (March) in a cold frame in rich soil, and kept well watered through its first year. Known as Gow Choy by the Chinese, it tastes like garlic.

Chives

Allium schoenprasum Very Hardy
Chives
get a root division from a friend or buy as bedding plant in spring (ABL has seeds)

Chives tend to die down in October/November, especially if it's a dry year. They then reappear in late February (or even earlier if you lift and force some in a sunny window), so I think they're worth having.

Fennel

Foeniculum vulgare Very Hardy
Fennel (ABL) or root division

Another perennial that is around for most of the year. It dies in October/November and then comes back up early in March. Not everyone will like its strong anise-like flavor, but if you do it's there waiting for you. I have seen quite a few wild plants in different parts of Seattle. They get very large (3 ft. in diameter, 4-5 ft. high), so be sure to put fennel where it won't interfere with your other herbs.

Sorrel

Rumex acetosa — Very Hardy
French Sorrel

R. acetosella — Very Hardy
Wild Sorrel (ABL)

R. scutatus — Hardy
Plain Sorrel (MB)

Wild Sorrel

Plain Sorrel French Sorrel

The sorrels impart a wonderful sour flavor to salads, but you pay for it with oxalic acid. I guess a certain amount of this doesn't hurt you, and if you aren't into lemons they are nice plants to have. Wild sorrel is a terrible "weed" on acid soils though, so watch it! I had a German roommate in high school who said her family made a soup of it during World War II called sauerumphe (or something like that). Sounds fun.

Garlic

Allium sativum Very Hardy
any variety

If you put garlic cloves in around October, they will put up green shoots just like onions. These are milder than the cloves, and go well in salads, sauces, omelets, etc. Separate the ones for cutting from your main garlic crop, however, as cutting robs the new cloves which are forming.

Horseradish

Armoracia rusticana Very Hardy
Horseradish (SGC)

You can dig the root of this crucifer all winter, if you remember to. In the spring, the pungent new leaves are a treat in salad. It's very easy to grow from a piece of root crown; in fact, it's hard to kill, so be sure to put it where it won't take over the rest of your perennial herbs.

Lovage

Levisticum officionales Very Hardy
Lovage (ABL,MB)

This member of the carrot/celery family is a perennial and has a wonderful original taste. It makes an early spring or fall salad, soup, or a sauce into something special. I got my plant by root division from a German winter gardener, Ute Grimlund of Marysville, Washington, but it apparently also comes easily from seed. Try and get seed fresh in that year; it ripens in July/August. The University of Washington Herb & Drug Plant garden has a nice bunch of plants.

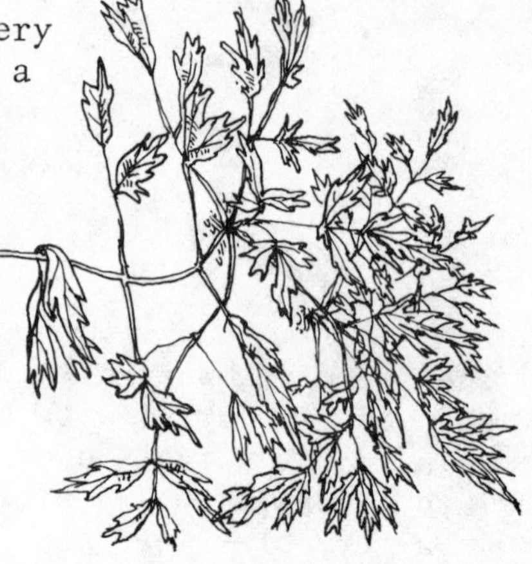

Oregano

Origanum spp. Hardy

The pink-flowered oregano, though tough and very hardy doesn't have much flavor.

Marjoram (*Origanum majorana*) usually has a very good flavor but, unfortunately, it is not hardy.

Rosemary

Rosmarinus officionalis Hardy (?)

Rosemary (from cuttings)

Best to get a start of this, put it in a fairly dry place, and water well till it's established. Rosemary is wonderful in winter stews, and small hints of it in salads are good, but best of all it makes a soothing tea after a harried excursion in the rain.

Sage

Salvia officionalis Very Hardy

Sage (from cuttings)

Most Americans know this in its dried form. It grows easily and you can have it fresh all winter too.

Salad Burnet

Sanguisorba minor Very Hardy
sometimes as: *Poterium sanguisorba*
Salad Burnet (ABL,H&H)

I feel that this is an herb of borderline usefulness. It certainly stays green throughout the winter, and it does taste of cucumbers, but rather bitter ones unfortunately. It isn't very succulent, but it does offer a nice variation in your winter salads, and it's supposed to be very good for you. To start it off, sow in spring or summer.

Skirret

Sium sisarum Hardy (?)
Skirret (ABL,H&H)

At the moment this is a mystery plant to me. It used to be grown in Europe. I haven't grown it yet, and am not sure how useful it is, or if the tops are available at all in the fall or winter. The root is, but seems to have a woody core, and not to be the sort of thing you'd want to spend time or garden space on. I include it as a curiosity. There are some skirret plants growing at the University of Washington Herb & Drug Plant Garden if you are interested.

Thyme - Lemon Thyme

Thymus vulgaris Very Hardy
Thyme (division or plants)

T. citriodorus varigatus
Lemon Thyme (division or plants)

Common thyme is easily found in many gardens, so you should be able to get a start easily. Lemon varigated thyme, which is so good in winter salads, is less common and you might have to search a little harder for it. It isn't as hardy, especially in its first two years, and might need mulching lightly in a cold site.

Winter Savory

Satureia montana Very Hardy
Winter Savory (division or seed-ABL)

This is a very strong flavored herb, and if you get to like it and plant it, it certainly will stay with you all winter long.

Some Cautionary Words

There are 62 vegetable and herb headings in this list, not counting the various varieties listed by seed companies. That's a lot. You certainly don't want to grow all of them at once. In fact, if it's your first year trying to carry crops through the coldest part of the winter, I suggest you try to limit yourself to five or six if you possibly can.

I know how hard it is when you get reading those seed catalogues in January—talk about temptation! But resist, for it does take a bit of forethought and several years experience before you can smoothly integrate your summer and winter gardening and become that well-fed person, the Year-Round Gardener.

If the winter part of gardening becomes a burden you are doing something wrong, for it should be a delightful gardening and culinary experience.

So go slow, and whatever else you do, sow and tend those plants with love!

Transformation 1

Knowing that nothing, not even the Earth you are standing on, is standing still, is part of the Earth-shelter-yoga. The more you feel these vibrations (the whole biosphere breathing as a lung and exchanging energy like the breath), the greater joy this more accurate and truthful Energy Earth will bring.

So find happiness in the fog, in mud, and dust. This is a plea not to indulge in criticism of the weather. As seashores sluff away and deserts turn to meadows, we are being entertained by the three states of matter that were the conditions for our life.

Peter Warshall

Appendices

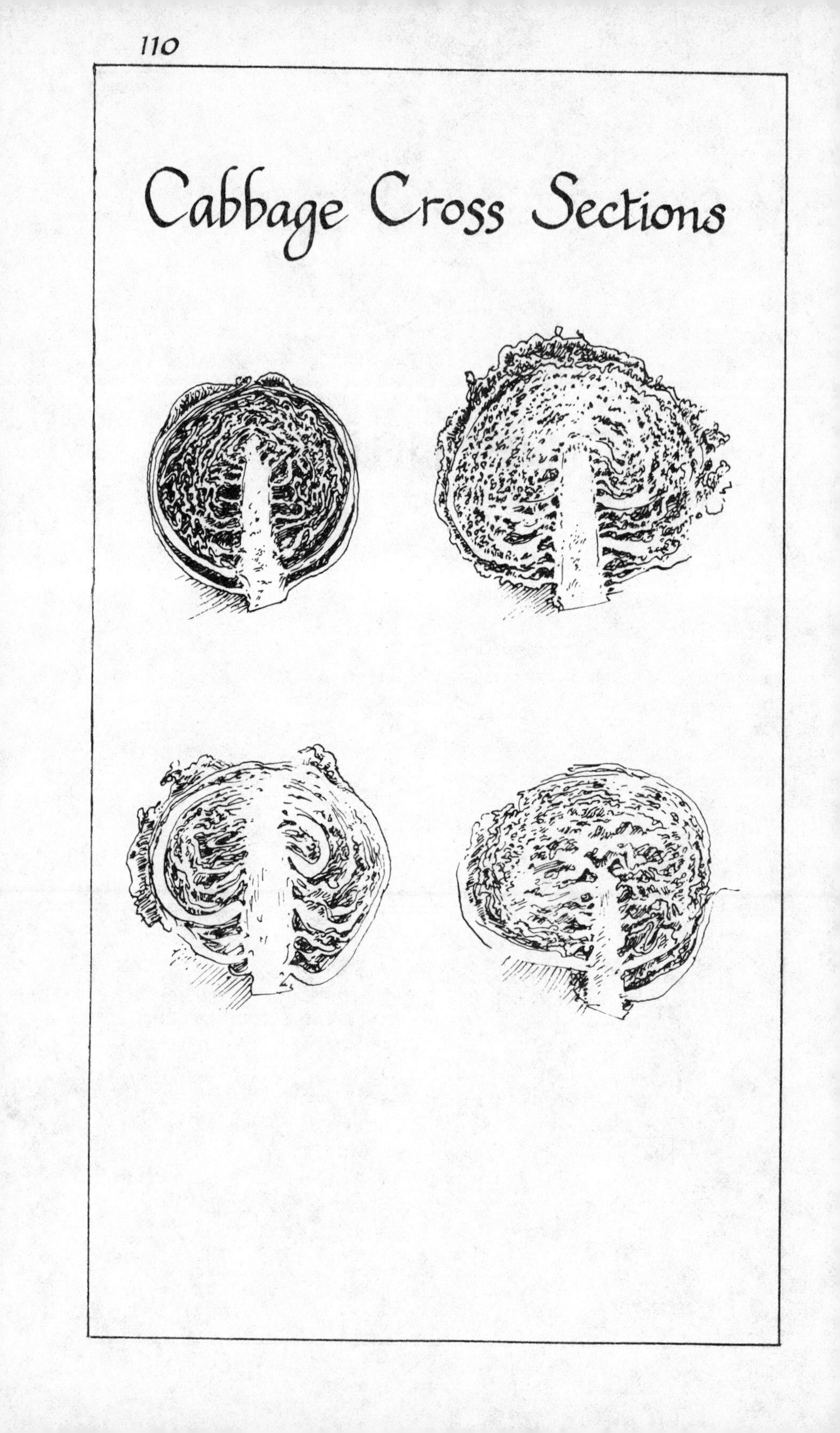
Cabbage Cross Sections

Commercial Production

As a gardener you are already taking some responsibility for your own food supply, which is good. But it is a very rare person in this country that can and wants to be totally self-sufficient in foodstuffs. We reach out for products from other climates and countries, increasing our dependence on the rest of the world.

I began growing winter vegetables because they were fresher than what I could find available for sale, and because I liked them better than peppers and tomatoes out of season. I agreed to begin telling others how to do it in part because I felt that the more gardeners we had growing winter vegetables and liking them, the more farmers would be able to grow and sell them.

In the process of researching about these vegetables and their cultural requirements, I discovered that, in the Maritime Northwest, we had the resources to grow our own winter foodstuffs. In addition, I discovered a whole world of self-reliance that had been developed by farmers and gardeners before the era of mass food production.

I began to see how and why our ability to feed ourselves had disintegrated in the face of growing control of our food supply by national and multi-national corporations. I began to see the need for building what Francis Moore Lappe and Joseph Collins call a democratically controlled and food self-reliant economy in America (see *World Hunger: Ten Myths*, page 128). And that, of course, means in the Maritime Northwest, too.

The Puget Consumers' Coop, which funded the original Winter Garden Project, did so in part because they saw a need for the production of fresh local foodstuffs. I began with gardening instead of farming because I am a gardener and because no one had made a recent catalogue of which vegetables and their varieties can be grown in our region through the winter. But now that this cataloguing task has been accomplished, it is time to turn to the task of producing winter vegetables on a larger scale.

Rebuilding local agriculture will be a major task because there has been a tremendous collapse of agriculture in the Maritime Northwest over the past thirty years. Over half a million acres of agricultural land have gone out of production in our region since World War II. From a region that was at one time nearly self-sufficient in fresh vegetables produced locally by small farmers, the Northwest has become dependent on the destructive forces of agribusiness.

In 1976, 1311 train carloads of fresh vegetables were imported into Portland, while another 2753 carloads were imported into Seattle. All of these vegetables were imported during times of the year when they could have been produced here. The land and the people of California, Texas, Florida and Mexico are all being exploited to provide us with "cheap" food, while in our own communities farmers are being forced off the land to make room for industry, highways, apartment houses and parking lots.

The task of agricultural reconstruction in the Maritime Northwest will be a massive one, but the development and practice of winter gardening may be one of the keys to helping us achieve this goal.

The economics of small-scale farming is hard at best. There are presently <u>no</u> easy ways to make a living as a small farmer, and the production of fresh market vegetables is one of the hardest ways of all. However, it is also one of the few ways to get a start in farming with only a few acres of land and limited capital. And it is also one of the few ways that you can directly compete economically with agribusiness.

High quality fresh market vegetables bring a premium price and there is an increasing demand for locally grown organic produce. There is a growing network of co-op and natural food stores that are committed to supporting local agriculture. By marketing through this alternative food system not only will your vegetables be worth more than the stuff shipped up from California but, if you employ organic methods, you will avoid the trap of skyrocketing inflation in all the petroleum-based fertilizers, herbicides and pesticides that chemical farms are totally addicted to.

Another key to successful small-scale farming is diversity, and this is where year-round vegetable production could play an increasingly important role. One primary element of the old agricultural economy was the assurance of always having something to sell or trade every week of the year, whether it was a dozen eggs, some garden produce, two gallons of milk, or some homespun cloth. For the market farmer a knowledge of winter gardening techniques could provide the diversity, and therefore the stability, needed to stay on the land.

Even if, like many small farmers, you must work off the farm during the winter in order to make the land payments and the taxes, there can always be something growing in the garden to feed your family and supplement your income. Leeks are easy to grow, are in great demand, and command a very good price. Brussels sprouts, if planted in late summer, will produce a crop for sale to local restaurants in February. There are late cabbages, such as January King, that will stand in the field for marketing in midwinter, while early varieties, such as Jersey Wakefield, can with luck and care be grown and harvested by April. Cauliflower is a difficult crop to grow, but Tommy Viloria, who farms in the Kent Valley, has beautiful ones for sale in Seattle's Pike Place Market in March. There's even a small but steady demand for fresh Jerusalem artichokes, one of the easiest of the winter crops.

The production of winter vegetables for market is hard work and very risky, which is why none of the big commercial operations ever chance it. In order to be successful you would need good land with a warm microclimate, and would need to be located a short distance from a reliable market. But even that won't be enough.

Farming can't survive in isolation. In a healthy culture, farming is an integral part of the whole community. Farmers are part of and are supported by the entire community. People understand the vital necessity of preserving agricultural land and of preserving the farmers on that land. The entire community shares a farmer's sensitive awareness of his or her environment. People eat what can be grown locally, when it can be grown, which means sweet corn in September and fresh, crisp kale for salads in February.

It may take a long while for the people of the Maritime Northwest to truly adopt a healthy culture and a regional diet, but education and the increasingly higher cost of trucked-in food will both work to the advantage of the year-round market farmer. In the years ahead winter gardening will become an increasingly important part of the revival of local agriculture.

Steps we can take to accomplish this include support programs to help keep farmers on the land and provide them with markets. Also needed is a program for research and education on winter vegetable production.

jersey wakefield

Winter Crops for Livestock

When I undertook the care of animals I was excited to find that there were as many foods available to them in the winter as there were to me. I discovered that hay, grain, and poor winter pasture were not the only possibilities for livestock. After doing some reading and after observing chickens, ducks, sheep, and goats through the winter, I began to understand that just as my diet had been restricted by the dictates of the supermarket, so had theirs by the local feed store and the recommendations of those who sell pasture mixtures.

I believe that the physical well-being of your livestock is certainly as important as your own, whether you keep a few rabbits and chickens in your backyard, or a flock of sheep, goats, or a cow on pasture. You have a special responsibility to provide for your animals. They are restrained from wandering at will and selecting from a wide range of vegetation what they need to meet the nutritional requirements of their yearly cycle.

Basically, as I see it, the problem is one of restoring lost habitat. Most of your livestock originated in Eurasia, and throughout their evolution fed on the vegetation of that area. The vegetation of the Maritime Northwest is *not* similar to that of mid-Europe. Our vegetation is mainly coniferous and it lacks many crucial elements for stock, such as abundant meadowlands, shrubbery and extensive deciduous woodlands, all diverse in plant (and animal) species.

When pastures were established in the Northwest, they were unavoidably created from mixtures bought at the store because pasture lands had not evolved naturally in this region. And hedgerows were not even considered at all. What's more, the pastures were being established during the rise of modern "scientific" agriculture, so the seed mixtures were monotypic, lacking in important forage plants, many of which would have been available throughout the winter.

What can you do to reverse this unhealthy trend for your stock? You can study the lists in this section and the books I have recommended and increase the diversity of the natural feed available for your animals. Not only will your animals be healthier, but in the end I think this approach could lower your feed costs since most of the feed sources I have listed are perennial plants.

I have divided the available winter feed into three categories: Succulents (such as kale); Pasture plants (herbs, legumes and grasses); and Browse (hedgerow plants with their buds, catkins, seeds, fruit and nuts). There is also hay, which is cut in summer and then stored for winter, and therefore out of the realm of this book, and a fifth category, termed "concentrates" by McKenzie, which I have omitted too, but which deserves some comment.

Concentrates are condensed proteins and carbohydrates, available in such foods as grains, soybeans, linseed cake, and other products of the feed industry. They are very rich and not all that suitable in the diets of animals except in small amounts or at particular stress points through the year. Browse in fact contains many of these concentrates in their wild natural form, especially in the fall, at mating time, and then again at birthing time when (if you allow your animals to birth naturally) most plant forms are again overflowing with spring sun energy.

Succulents

Succulents include all the leavings of your garden, and specially planted stock foods such as Marrowstem and Thousand-Headed kale, mangles (stock beets), sugar beets, turnips, rutabagas and carrots. The roots are mostly suitable for ruminants, but the leavings of your garden and the kales are liked by poultry, rabbits and pigs as well. Succulents can provide a source of fresh vegetable feed for your animals throughout the winter.

Pasture

If you are raising livestock on an average Northwest pasture you will want to renovate it as soon as you have money and time. When you do this you can simply include as many herb seeds as you can gather up to place with the grasses and clover you choose.

These greatly increase the forage and hay available to your stock during the most stressful times of the year—winter and early spring. Many herbs are deep rooted and collect minerals that grasses and clovers do not, reducing the need for mineral supplements. They are a real asset and are well worth the extra expense of the seed and the extra effort required to seek them out.

The three best authorities that I know on the subject of herbs and pastures are David McKenzie, *Goat Husbandry*, Newman Turner, *Fertility Pastures*, and J. de Bairacli Levy, *Herbal Handbook for Farm and Stable*. The Levy and Turner books give lists of plants especially beneficial to different stock. Turner deals mostly with common herbs ("weeds") and their role in pastures. Levy deals with the more medicinal plants for hedgerows and pastures. See the Sources section for complete references for these books.

This is what McKenzie has to say on the importance of herbs in pastures:

> For centuries we have been feeding our sheep and cattle on a mixture of grass, legumes, and miscellaneous fodder plants, including weeds such as daisy, buttercup and nettle, acceptable meadow species like plantain and yarrow, and cultivated pasture plants like chicory and burnet. During all of that time every farmer who wasn't stone blind knew his stock ate most of them and liked them. Until relatively recently he maintained these species on his fields by sowing out with barn sweepings. Since the introduction of pedigree seeds mixtures, the average annual hay crop has shown no significant increase, the sale of mineral mixtures for stock-feeding has risen from near zero to over 40,000 tons per annum, and mineral deficiency disease has become a major farm problem. The effect of replacing these miscellaneous pasture plants by grass and clover is to reduce the mineral content of the sward by approximately 20 per cent.
>
> No special inspiration or insight into the Workings of Nature is needed to reach these conclusions. Brynmor Thomas and fellow research workers at the Durham University School of Agriculture have investigated accurately the earlier suggestions of R. H. Elliott and Stapledon. Here are the facts concerning one of their trial fields at Cockle Park.

The Percentage Composition of the Herbage from Swards Containing Varying Percentages of Other Fodder Plants

Constituent	*Standard Grass and Clover Mixture*	*With 10% Other Fodder Plants*	*With 50% Other Fodder Plants*	*With 100% Other Fodder Plants*
Crude protein	16·75	17·19	16·90	16·94
Crude fibre	21·32	19·49	18·61	15·16
Total ash	10·18	11·07	13·01	14·83
Calcium	1·15	1·36	1·60	2·16
Phosphorus	0·29	0·36	0·38	0·41
Magnesium	0·42	0·45	0·48	0·52
Sodium	0·08	0·11	0·14	0·18
Chlorine	0·26	0·30	0·37	0·48

David McKenzie, *Goat Husbandry*, pp 153, 157.

Hedgerows

Hedgerows are a form of fence, and they are best used as such. Aside from their nutritional aspects, they provide shelter from the wind for your stock and wildings. They are also a year-long entrancement for plants, birds, insects, reptiles and animals to help increase the diversity of your local biota.

If your fences are already up you can till or disc along the human side of them, put in your rooted cuttings and sow your herbs. Put the plants just far enough from the fence so that the animals can't reach them when they stick their heads through. This way the plantings will survive to get big enough to grow through the fence, and then the stock will keep them clipped on that side.

You will have to trim the tops and side branches on the human side of your hedgerows whenever you have time or when your pastures are such that the animals will benefit from the extra rations. Heavy pruning makes the hedge more dense. Seymour's *Guide to Self-Sufficiency* has a description on how to make a planted hedge stockproof (see Sources).

I list below a few shrub species, both local and imported, that are most useful in the edible winter hedge. The starred ones are recommended by McKenzie as especially good for cool seasons. You can also use your imagination or read up in Levy's *Herbal Handbook for Farm and Stable* to see what else would be good. Don't forget roses! And make sure you don't include poisonous plants such as rhododendrons.

If you are short of cash, buy some clippers and Rootone, read up on propagating by cuttings and, as you drive around or visit friends, keep your eyes trained on the shrubbery. Most folks who have a nice plant of some kind are only too happy to share a few clippings with you.

HEDGE PLANTS FOR THE MARITIME NORTHWEST

This list omits many plant varieties good for summer use. Asterisk * indicates good midwinter plant.

Plant Sources—see page 123 for addresses
Valley Nursery (VN), MsK Nursery (MsK)

APPLE/CRABAPPLE *Malus sp.* The fruits are very good for stock in the fall.

ASH* *Fraxinus sp.* There is a native Oregon Ash which is rare in Washington but seems to grow in every swale of the Willamette Valley. If you live up north and have trouble finding seedlings, you can buy one of the Eastern species from a nursery. (VN,MsK)

BIRCH *Betula occidentalis* Native hedge plant in Eastern Washington. Good for spring and fall. (MsK)

BLACKTHORN *Prunus spinosa* European. Buy from a nursery or get cuttings from friends.

BLUEBERRY *Vaccinium sp.* If you have your own blueberry plants, you can make summer cuttings for the hedge rows rather easily. Wild blueberries are good too. They can be found in the Cascade foothills.

BRAMBLES *Rubus sp.* Raspberries and blackberries. If you do plant these, remember that they spread like mad and have to be controlled. At least get good fruiting varieties; thornless would be good. Use starts from your own plants if you have them. Good for winter and early spring.

ELDER *Sambucus nigra* Native east of the Cascades. Get seed, or try root divisions or seedlings.

ELM* *Ulmus sp.* Siberian Elm is probably the best. (VN)

HAWTHORN *Crataegus monogyna, C. oxycanthus* European and native species available. Get ones that fruit readily. Cuttings are easy. The Northwest native is *C. douglasii*. (VN?)

HAZEL *Corylus cornuta* A native that can be found everywhere. Highly nutritious; good in early spring, February/March. A relative of Filberts, *C. avellana*. (MsK)

HEATHER* *Erica sp.* English, but horticultural varieties available from nurseries. Excellent from autumn to midwinter.

HOLLY* *Ilex aquifolium* English, but common here as both an ornamental and a commercial crop. Goats devour it with glee all winter (and summer too!).

HONEYSUCKLE *Lonicera periclymenum*-introduced. Good goat fare; makes hedge denser by twining through it. This is the common sweet smelling honeysuckle so often planted. Cuttings are easy. Goats might also like the orange flavored native, *L. ciliosa*. (MsK)

HUCKLEBERRY *Vaccinium ovatum* Common Evergreen Huckleberry. Bears dark blue berries till Christmas. Common on Vashon Island in deep woods. Red Huckleberry, *V. parvifolium*, is common in the foothills growing from old cedar stumps. Sheep like the leaves. (MsK)

IVY* *Hedera helix* Imported; common and easy to start, but hard to get rid of! Good all winter.

MOUNTAIN ASH *Sorbus spp.* Sheep like the leaves; ducks, chickens, and wild birds like the berries. (MsK)

WILLOW* *Salix sp.* The many native types all provide good winter feed for cows, sheep, and goats. The earliest blooming willows give bee forage in February.

Sources

Seeds

I wish I could tell you that you can order from one place all the seeds for the plants I've discussed, but no such luck. What's more, new varieties no doubt will be coming out each year, so you will be faced with that also. I always enjoy going through the first catalogue of the year, but by the time I'm through the tenth, I feel strangely crazy and want to forget the whole thing. That's where restraint is a help, and I urge you to practice it if you can!

Many of the winter garden seeds you'll be ordering will come from Europe. For overseas ordering, use an International Money Order; don't try to figure the currency yourself or send a personal check. Go to a bank and get an International Money Order.

And note: do not buy untreated pea and bean seed from the East Coast, since they tend to carry diseases which can devastate your crop. We have had bad luck this way at Pragtree Farm, two years running now.

SOURCES FOR SEEDS

Abundant Life Seed Foundation, Box 374, Gardiner WA 98334.

Catalogue 50¢. Untreated seed, no hybrids. Locally grown seed where possible. Sold throughout the food coop system, or ordered directly. Will do trades, pass on information, etc. Good folk.

Alexander & Brown, Box 13, South Methven St., Per Perth, Scotland PH1 5NY.

Their catalogue came too late for me to order from this year, but they definitely look worthwhile, Scottish weather being what it is.

Five Corners Nurseries and Hardware, Inc., 15826 1st Ave. S., Seattle WA. 206/242-2931.
If you live in the south end of Seattle, this is your first stop for winter vegetable seeds.

Herbs & Honey, Rt 2, Box 205, Monmouth OR 97361.
Unusual hardy herbs, of good quality. No deliveries; you must pick up your order. Abundant Life carries some of their seeds.

Johnny's Selected Seeds, Albion ME 04910.
Catalogue 50¢. Untreated, no hybrids. Many grown on their own farm. Interesting European varieties. Very reliable...more good folk. Booklet, *Growing Garden Seeds*, very helpful.

Meadowbrook Herb Garden, Wyoming RI 02898.
Seeds for unusual herb varieties. These folk grow biodynamically, their greenhouse is amazing, and the emphasis is on quality (with the unfortunate corollary of high price).

Seattle Garden Center, Pike Place Market, Seattle WA 98101.
Owner Bob Gill has been helping year-round gardeners for many years. They carry lots of treated seeds, so if you care about this, inquire before you buy.

Chase Compost Seeds Ltd., Banhall, Saxmundham, London, England.

Stokes Seeds, Box 548, Buffalo NY 14240.
Wide selection, commercial varieties, much Canadian seed. The Burpee of the North, but better and cheaper. Ask for untreated (UT) if you care.

Suttons Seeds, Hele Rd, Torquay, Devon, England.
Many winter varieties; reasonable prices.

Thompson & Morgan, Box 100, Farmingdale NJ 07727.
US outlet for the British firm of the same name. Very interesting catalogue, some hokey, very expensive, but worth it for those few varieties you can't get elsewhere. They prepare a summer catalogue, but I would order what you need all at once in the spring.

Tillinghast Seeds, La Conner WA 98257.
A few good winter coles.

True Seed Exchange, c/o Kent Whealy, RFD 2 (TN), Princeton MO 64673.

Members get a list, organized by state, of those who wish to share the seeds they have in exchange for other varieties. There are already some maritime Northwest members. Costs a dollar.

Tsang & Ma International, Box 294, Belmont CA 94002.

Interesting Asian varieties. Some can be found at Seattle Garden Center.

Vilmorin-Andrieux, c/o J.A. Demonchaux Co, 827 North Kansas, Topeka KS 66608.

Vilmorin-Andrieux carries an interesting collection of French varieties, many for over-wintering.

William Dam, West Flamboro, Ontario, Canada LOR 2KO.

Some good, cheap unusual varieties for winter. Stock varieties also.

SOURCES FOR PLANTS

MsK Rare and Native Plant Nursery, 20066 15th NW, Seattle WA 98117. 206/546-1281.

Mareen S. Kruckeberg (MsK) collects native plants. She gathers them in the wild from cuttings, seedlings and seeds, and propagates them in her home nursery. Her catalogue lists over 140 different native trees and shrubs, and it is available without charge.

Her husband, Arthur Kruckeberg, is president of the Washington Native Plant Society. The Society's goal is to discover and preserve rare and endangered plant species in this region. More information on the Society is available from Mr. Kruckeberg, c/o University of Washington Botany Dept., Seattle WA 98195.

Valley Nursery, Box 4845, Helena MT 58601

The Valley Nursery provides very hardy and inexpensive trees and shrubs in bulk amounts (10s and 100s).

Books You Should Read

Better Vegetable Gardens the Chinese Way by Peter Chan and Spencer Gill. 1977. Graphic Arts Center, Portland, Oregon.

The authors have a wry sense of humor that appeals to me, and the photographs show another culture's version of raised permanent beds. Rather expensive; maybe you can find it in a library. Not much winter cropping information.

Earth Market by Wendy Bender, Box 496, Sooke, British Columbia, Canada VOS 1NO.

Very good local book (Sooke is about the same latitude as Mt. Vernon, Washington, regardless of "national boundaries"), that gives a good feeling for gardening on coastal Vancouver Island. Some general cultural information and recipes.

The Food Lover's Garden by A.M. Pellegrini. 1975 reprint. Madrona Publishers, 113 Madrona Place East, Seattle WA 98112.

Discursive, interesting book by excellent Seattle gardener, with general cultural information, recipes, etc. Had it been more complete in the fall and winter section, I wouldn't have bothered to write this book.

Grow Your Own Fruits & Vegetables by L.D. Hills. 1975. Faber & Faber, 3 Queen Square, London WC1, England.

For more experienced gardeners. Certainly the most erudite of the recent English gardening books. Hills is director of the Henry Doubleday Research Association, Bocking, Braintree, Essex, England. Well worth joining.

The New Vegetable Growers Handbook by A.J. Simons. 1975 Edition, Penguin Books, 2801 John St, Markham, Ontario, Canada L3R IB4. 306 pp.

Although this book was written for British gardeners, the cultural directions are applicable to most northern maritime winter gardens. They are the most basic and complete that I have seen in a modern book. You will only have to adapt your planting dates.

Send orders attention Brian Cooney. Approximately $4.50 plus duty, payable on receipt. Bookstores have had trouble ordering this book from US and British outlets, so have your bookstore order from the Penguin outlet in Canada (or you can do it yourself).

The Complete Vegetable Growers Handbook by W.E. Shewell-Cooper. 1975. Faber & Faber, 3 Queen Square, London, WC1, England. Useful for maritime growers.

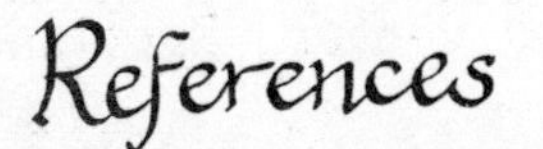

Bio-Dynamic Agriculture by H.H. Koepf, B.D. Petterson and W. Shaumann. 1976. Anthroposophic Press, distributed by Bio-Dynamic Literature, Box 253, Wyoming RI 02898. 429pp. $12.

This is a long book, but maybe the best for getting a good sense of what Bio-Dynamics is about. Their preparations are designed to produce plants that would tend towards cold-hardiness.

The City Peoples' Book of Raising Food by Helga and William Olkowski. Rodale Press, Emmaus PA 18049.

Excellent book, with many well-researched, intelligent ideas from the Bay Area. Worth reading, even if you live in the country. Rodale Press, at the above address, publishes lots of good books on organic gardening and self-sufficiency, as well as the monthly magazine *Organic Gardening & Farming*.

Cole Crops: Botany, Cultivation & Utilization by M. Nieuwhof. 1969. Leonard Hill Co, London, England.

Very textbooky, but some revealing information on the more common of the coles. Good if you have to write a term paper and need a reference. Lots of data from studies on cold, pests, manuring, etc.

Common Herbs for Natural Health by Juliette de Bairacli Levy. 1974. Schocken Books, New York. (pbk)

Companion Plants by Helen Philbrick & Richard Gregg. St. George Book Service, Box 225, Spring Valley NY 10977.

This is the book that so many people quote when they say that certain plants grow well together and others don't. I guess you should make your own experiments before you take it too seriously.

The Guide to Self-Sufficiency by John Seymour. 1976. Popular Mechanics Books.

This looks to be a bit flashy, but has lots of hard core information. The American edition is done specifically for the USA. I think I would rather own the British edition (though I haven't seen it) since, generally, anything written for the USA ignores the Northwest Coast like a plague, and our growing conditions are more like England and Europe than Minnesota or Massachusetts.

The Complete Vegetable Grower by W.E. Sherwell-Cooper. Faber & Faber, 3 Queen Square, London WC1, England.
Pretty good, but not up to Simons except in general gardening directions.

Farming for Self-Sufficiency by John & Sally Seymour. Schocken Books, New York.
Excellent if you have five acres or more (or less!). The original subsistence folk of Britain, their current farm is in Wales.

Fertility Pastures by Newman Turner.
A reprint of this 1955 Faber & Faber classic is available from Rateaver, Pauma Valley CA 92061.

Goat Husbandry by David Mackenzie. 1956. Faber & Faber, 3 Queen Square, London WC1, England.
Another of their classic alternative agriculture books. Fantastic scope and detail, worth it even if you don't have goats. Pertinent to the care of any grazing animal.

Growing Vegetables in the Pacific Northwest by Cecil Solly. Madrona Publishers, Seattle WA. Out of print.
Wartime goody, dated only in some varieties and chemical advice. Second edition, available at the University Branch of the Seattle Public Library, is the best, since it has monthly garden maps, showing what to sow, transplant, and harvest.

Five Acres & Independence by Kains & McClure.
A 1973 reprint is available from NAL Publishers, New York.

Herbal Handbook for Farm & Stable by Juliette de Bairacli Levy. 1952. Faber & Faber, 3 Queen Square, London WC1, England.
A Rodale Press paperback reprint is available in this country. An invaluable aid to weaning yourself and your stock from standard allopathic Western medicine.

How to Grow More Vegetables by John Jeavons. Ecology Action of the Midpeninsula, 2225 El Camino Real, Palo Alto CA 94306.
Devoted to the "biodynamic French Intensive" method.

Improving Garden Soils with Green Manure by Alther and Raymond. Garden Way Publications, Charlotte VT 05445.

Onion Production by Donald Comin. 1946. Orange Judd Publishers, New York.

Organic Gardening Under Glass by Abraham & Abraham. Rodale Press, Emmaus PA 18049.
Very complete and helpful suggestions. Unfortunately, due to our low light levels, some of their vegetable suggestions don't work very well during the darkest part of our winter.

The Organic Method Primer by Rateaver & Rateaver, Pauma Valley CA 92061.
Good overview and thorough approach to subject.

Oxford Book of Food Plants by Harrison, Masefield and Wallis. 1969. Oxford University Press, Ely House, London W1, England.
Good reference, gorgeous illustrations. I used this for Latin nomenclature.

Sensitive Chaos: The Creation of Flowing Forms in Water & Air by Theodor Schwenk. 1965. Rudolf Steiner Press, London, England. Available from Steiner Book Center, Inc., 151 Carisbrooke Crescent, North Vancouver, British Columbia, Canada V7N 2S2.
If you want some insights into a side of water and air that we aren't usually taught to observe, read a and look at this book.

Slugs & the Garden. 1963. Henry Doubleday Research Assn., Bockingham, Braintree, Essex, England.

Solar Greenhouse by Fisher & Yanda. John Muir Publications, Santa Fe NM 97501. Available from Bookpeople, 2940 Seventh St., Berkeley CA 94710.
This book covers greenhouse growing, a topic I don't discuss in this book.

Solar Survival Press. Harrisville NH 03450.

Vegetable Crops by Thompson & Kelly. McGraw Hill, Novato CA. Good textbook.

The Vegetable Garden by Madame Vilmorin-Andrieux. Jeavons-Leler Press, 855 Clara Drive, Palo Alto CA 94303.

Originally published in Paris in 1860, this is a reprint of the 1920 English edition. I got a hold of a 1920 copy and, as Woody Deryckx said, it's rather like reading a seed catalogue from Mars. Fully 80 percent of the varieties must be extinct by this time. Still, the cultural sections that precede the variety listings are very interesting, coming as they do from another age. Reading them will, at the very least, broaden your concept of how to garden.

Weather-Wise Gardening, West Edition. 1974. Ortho Books.

Some very good graphically-presented climate control information, interspersed with plugs for plastic and other petroleum products. If you can ignore the latter, buy the book at your local chain hardware store.

Wild Flowers of Britain & Northern Europe by Fitter and Belamey. 1974. Scribner & Sons, New York.

Building and Using Our Sun Heated Greenhouse by Helen and Scott Nearing. 1977. Garden Way Publishing, Charlotte VT 05445. A very good book for New England winter gardeners. Simple, straight forward, and real.

World Hunger: Ten Myths by Frances Moore Lappe and Joseph Collins. 1977. Institute for Food & Development Policy, 2588 Mission St., San Francisco CA 94110.

Tools

CLOCHES

The Guard 'n Gro Cloche Co., 61 Cromary Way, Inverness CA 94937.

Very expensive ($19.95 per 42-inch x 18-inch x 21-inches high section), but handy if you want one. Not tested.

Solar Survival, Harrisville NH 03450.

Excellent cloche design.